Grades K & Up
Ages 5 & Up

Functional Sequencing Activity Sheets
for Daily Living Skills

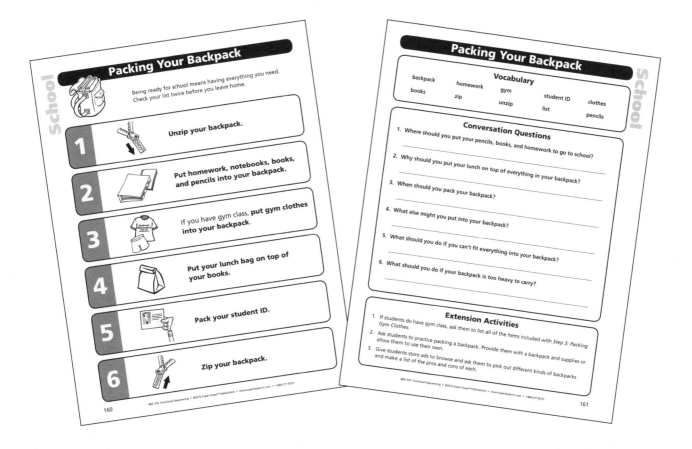

by Candy Schraufnagel and Amy Crimin, M.S. Ed., MS. Psy.

Edited by Becky Spivey, M.Ed.; Liz Wright, MAPC; and Jessica Horton

Printed in the United States

ISBN 978-1-58650-984-2

Super Duper® Publications
www.superduperinc.com
1-800-277-8737

Introduction

Functional Sequencing provides six-step sequences for daily living activities. There are basic activities such as getting dressed, washing hands, and eating dinner up to more complex activities such as packing a lunch, eating at a buffet, and going to the movie theater.

These sequences are useful and practical for teaching how to do an activity as well as reinforcing and reassuring a student that he/she is doing an activity correctly. These sequences are not steadfast; feel free to adapt them to your student's specific needs.

On the page opposite the six steps, there are ten vocabulary words that help to enrich and extend the lesson. Six conversation questions follow the vocabulary words to help students comprehend why we do certain things in the six steps. Some of the steps may seem too simple to include, but remember it is part of the sequencing of events and vital in recalling the steps in the functional sequence.

Three extension activities follow the vocabulary and conversation questions. These extension activities may or may not be applicable to your population of students; however, they will give you ideas that you can adapt specifically for your students.

Print any of the workbook pages in black and white or full color using the included CD-ROM. Send the Parent/Helper Letter (p. vi) home with worksheets for even more practice. The blank sequence template (p. vii) lets you create your own sequence for any activity. Present students with award certificates (p. viii) as they master sequences!

Activity Ideas

1. Cut apart the six sequence steps. Mix up the steps and ask students to put them in the correct order. To simplify for lower-level students, remove some of the steps so they only have to put together two-, three-, or four-step sequences.

2. List one of the key words from each step on the board. Ask students to put the words in order based on the steps in the sequence. For example, for eating at a fast-food restaurant you might write words like sit, order, choose, throw, eat, and wait. The students would order as *choose, wait, order, sit, eat, throw*.

3. Give each student a step. Have students work together to put themselves in the correct order.

4. Give each student a step. Ask them to draw their own pictures to represent the steps.

Contents

Meal Time 1–21

Hygiene............................ 23–43

Household Chores 45–65

Safety.................................. 67–81

#BK-376 Functional Sequencing • ©2010 Super Duper® Publications • www.superduperinc.com • 1-800-277-8737

Contents

Parent/Helper Letter

Date: _____

Dear Parent/Helper:

Your child is currently working on _____ .

The attached worksheet(s) will help your child practice and reinforce skills reviewed in the classroom.

☐ After you complete these exercises with your child, please sign and return them by _____.

☐ Please complete these exercises with your child. You do not need to return them to me.

☐ _____
_____
_____

Thank you for your support.

_____   _____
Teacher/Speech-Language Pathologist   Parent/Helper Signature

#BK-376 Functional Sequencing • ©2010 Super Duper® Publications • www.superduperinc.com • 1-800-277-8737

1	
2	
3	
4	
5	
6	

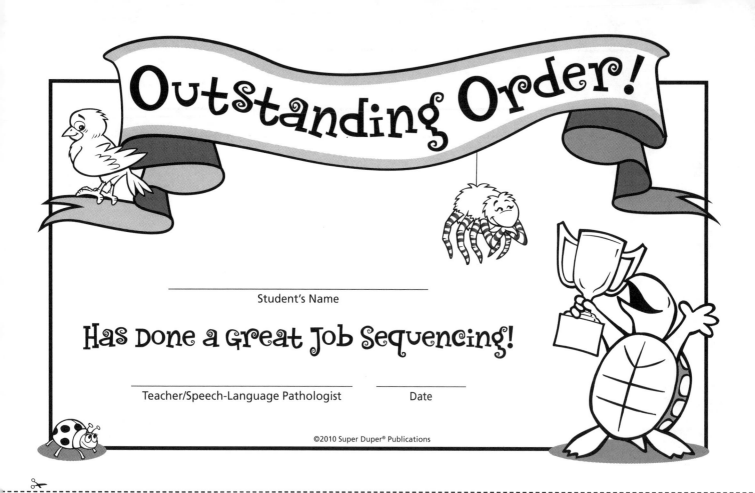

Outstanding Order!

_____
Student's Name

Has Done a Great Job Sequencing!

_____   _____
Teacher/Speech-Language Pathologist   Date

©2010 Super Duper® Publications

SEQUENCING SUPERSTAR!

IS A

_____
Student's Name

_____   _____
Teacher/Speech-Language Pathologist   Date

©2010 Super Duper® Publications

Meal Time

Meals at Home

Eating meals at home with your family is a great way to spend time together.

1		**Set the table.** Put a plate, glass, silverware, and napkin at each seat.
2		**Sit down at the table** and lay your napkin on your lap.
3		**Serve yourself** the foods on the table.
4		**Eat your food.** Ask for a second helping if you are still hungry.
5		**Take your dishes to the sink** when you finish eating.
6		**Help clean up** by wiping off the table.

#BK-376 Functional Sequencing • ©2010 Super Duper® Publications • www.superduperinc.com • 1-800-277-8737

Meals at Home

Vocabulary

hungry	silverware	finish	clean up	sink
table	serve	family	helping	napkin

Conversation Questions

1. Which meals do you eat with your family?

   _____

2. What is your favorite meal?

   _____

3. What do you do if you want a food that you can't reach?

   _____

4. What should you do with your napkin while you are eating?

   _____

5. What should you do if you are still hungry?

   _____

6. Why is it important to wipe off the table after you eat?

   _____

Extension Activities

1. Discuss the proper way to set a table. Give each student a fork, spoon, knife, cup, plate, napkin, etc. Ask students to set the table.

2. Ask students to list good table manners. Write them on the board. Ask students to practice good manners while eating lunch.

3. Hold up a fork, knife, spoon, salad plate, etc., and ask students to tell you how to use each one. Discuss the answers as a class.

Dinner at a Friend's House

Going to your friend's house for dinner is fun. When your friend invites you for dinner, make sure to let him or her know if you can go. Ask what time you should arrive. Don't be late!

1

Offer to help set the table. Put a plate, glass, silverware, and napkin at each seat.

2

Sit down at the table and lay your napkin on your lap.

3

Serve yourself the foods on the table.

4

Eat your food. Ask for a second helping if you are still hungry.

5

Take your dishes to the sink when you finish eating.

6

Thank your friend for having you over for dinner.

#BK-376 Functional Sequencing • ©2010 Super Duper® Publications • www.superduperinc.com • 1-800-277-8737

Dinner at a Friend's House

Vocabulary

friend	time	guest	food	thank
dinner	invite	set	plate	eat

Conversation Questions

1. What should you do when a friend invites you over for dinner?

   _____

2. How do you know where to sit at a friend's house?

   _____

3. Why should you offer to help with the dishes?

   _____

4. What should you do if you don't like the dinner at your friend's house?

   _____

5. How should you dress for dinner at a friend's house?

   _____

6. What should you do if you are late for dinner at a friend's house?

   _____

Extension Activities

1. Ask students to pretend to invite each other over for dinner. Have them accept or decline the invitation. Discuss how each answer makes them feel.

2. Ask students to plan a menu as if they have friends coming over for dinner. Have them draw a plate with the food on it.

3. There are many ways to spend time with friends. Have students list other activities that they can do with their friends.

Dine-In Restaurant

Restaurant Name:_____

Address:_____

Phone Number: _____

1  **Tell the host or hostess your name** and how many people will be sitting with you.

2  When your name is called, follow the host or hostess and **sit down at the table**.

3  **Look at the menu and choose the food you want to order** including your drink, meal, and sides.

4  **Tell the server what you would like to eat.** Wait patiently for your food to come.

5  **Eat your food.** If you have leftovers, you may ask for a to-go box.

6  The server will bring you your check. **Pay for your meal** and tip your server.

#BK-376 Functional Sequencing • ©2010 Super Duper® Publications • www.superduperinc.com • 1-800-277-8737

Dine-In Restaurant

Vocabulary

hostess	server	tip	restaurant	eat
name	menu	dine-in	host	patient

Conversation Questions

1. Why should you tell the host or hostess your name and how many people will be sitting with you?

   _____

2. Why do you tip at a dine-in restaurant?

   _____

3. Do you have to clean the table at a dine-in restaurant? Why or why not?

   _____

4. What should you do if you don't know what something is on the menu?

   _____

5. Why should you wait for everyone to get their food before you start eating?

   _____

6. What does a hostess do?

   _____

Extension Activities

1. Have students pretend they are at a dine-in restaurant. Have one student be the host or hostess, another the customer, another the server, etc. Let them switch roles and say what's different about each role.

2. Give students a menu from a restaurant. Tell them that they only have $20 to spend and ask what they would order.

3. Have students create menus for their own restaurants.

Buffet-Style Restaurant

Meal Time

Restaurant Name: _____

Address: _____

Phone Number: _____

1  **Tell the host or hostess your name** and how many people will be sitting with you.

2  When your name is called, follow the host or hostess and **sit down at the table**.

3  **Tell the server what you would like to drink.**

4  At the buffet, pick up a plate. **Serve yourself** the foods on the buffet.

5  **Eat your food.** If you want more food, leave your dirty plate on the table and repeat Step 4.

6  The server will bring you your check. **Pay for your meal** and tip your server.

#BK-376 Functional Sequencing • ©2010 Super Duper® Publications • www.superduperinc.com • 1-800-277-8737

Buffet-Style Restaurant

Vocabulary

buffet	drink	dirty	hostess	serve
line	clean	plate	glass guards	germs

Conversation Questions

1. How is food served at a buffet?

   _____

2. Why do you get a clean plate each time you visit the buffet?

   _____

3. How do you feel if you eat too much food?

   _____

4. Buffets often have glass guards over the food; why do you think this is?

   _____

5. Why is it extra important to wash your hands before and after eating at a buffet?

   _____

6. What does wanting seconds or thirds mean?

   _____

Extension Activities

1. Discuss germs with students and how germs are spread. Ask students what role germs may play at a buffet-style restaurant.

2. Buffets often serve a variety of foods. Have students draw plates of food they would serve themselves at a buffet.

3. Have each student bring in a snack for the class. Place them all on a table. Have students pretend they are at a buffet.

Fast-Food Restaurant

Meal Time

Restaurant Name: _____

Address: _____

Phone Number: _____

1  **Look at the menu and choose what you want to order** including drink, meal, and sides.

2  **Wait in line** for the cashier.

3  **Tell the cashier what you would like to eat.** The cashier will tell you how much it will cost.

4  **Pay for your meal.** Step to the side while you wait for your food.

5  Find a place to sit and **eat your food**.

6  **Throw your trash away** when you finish eating.

#BK-376 Functional Sequencing • ©2010 Super Duper® Publications • www.superduperinc.com • 1-800-277-8737

Fast-Food Restaurant

Vocabulary

meal	same	cashier	manners	fast-food
line	condiments	sit	different	sides

Conversation Questions

1. What are four fast-food restaurants in your area?

   _____

2. What kinds of foods can you get at fast-food restaurants?

   _____

3. Why is it important to step to the side while you wait for your food?

   _____

4. Should your table manners be the same or different when you are eating fast food versus eating at home?

   _____

5. How do you tell the cashier that you don't want certain condiments on your food?

   _____

6. What should you do if you spill your drink?

   _____

Extension Activities

1. Put together a fast-food station with paper cutouts of food (lettuce, cheese, burgers, buns). Ask each student to make a burger. Discuss the differences between the burgers.

2. Print out the nutritional information for local fast-food restaurants. Discuss nutrition with the students and ask them to order a healthy meal from each of the restaurants.

3. Give students a menu from a fast-food restaurant. Tell them that they only have $10 to spend and ask what they would order.

Drive-Thru Restaurant

Restaurant Name: _____

Address: _____

Phone Number: _____

1  **Roll down your window and drive up to the speaker.**

2  **Look at the menu and choose what you want to order.**

3  **Tell the cashier what you would like to eat** by talking into the speaker.

4  **Drive up to the next window and pay for your meal.**

5  **Take your food and drink.**

6  **Roll up the window and drive to the nearest parking spot to park.**

 #BK-376 Functional Sequencing • ©2010 Super Duper® Publications • www.superduperinc.com • 1-800-277-8737

Drive-Thru Restaurant

Vocabulary

roll down	drive-thru	park	repeat	change
window	speaker	drive	pay	choose

Conversation Questions

1. Why shouldn't someone eat and drive at the same time?

   _____

2. What should you do if the cashier repeats your order and it's not what you want?

   _____

3. What should you do with your trash when you finish eating?

   _____

4. Why can't you walk through a drive-thru?

   _____

5. What should you do if the cashier gives you the wrong change?

   _____

6. What are some safety rules to follow while in a drive-thru or restaurant parking lot?

   _____

Extension Activities

1. Ask students to pretend they are taking orders at the drive-thru. How should they greet customers? What should they be doing after they take the customer's order?

2. Ask the students to draw a picture of a car in a drive-thru.

3. Why should you or the driver of the car park after getting food? Discuss traffic safety with students.

Food To Go

Meal Time

Restaurant Name: _____

Address: _____

Phone Number: _____

1  **Choose what you want to order** including your drink.

2  **Call the restaurant** and let the cashier know that you have a to-go order.

3  **Tell the cashier your name and order your food.** The cashier will tell you when to pick up your food.

4  **Go to the restaurant.**

5  **Tell the cashier you have a to-go order and your name. Pay the cashier.**

6  **Take the food home.**

#BK-376 Functional Sequencing • ©2010 Super Duper® Publications • www.superduperinc.com • 1-800-277-8737

Food To Go

Vocabulary

to-go	coupon	order	place	cashier
borrow	take	manners	wrong	pick up

Conversation Questions

1. **Why would you place a to-go order?**

   _____

2. **Do you need to leave a tip for to-go orders?**

   _____

3. **Where can you find the menu for a restaurant?**

   _____

4. **What kinds of food does your family order to go?**

   _____

5. **What should you do if your order is wrong?**

   _____

6. **Where can you find coupons for to-go restaurants?**

   _____

Extension Activities

1. Ask students to brainstorm other reasons why you would order something ahead of time.

2. Have one student pretend to be the cashier and one student pretend to call in a large order. See who can get the order 100% correct.

3. Discuss good phone manners with students. Have them practice their best phone manners.

Pizza Delivery

Restaurant Name: _____

Address: _____

Phone Number: _____

1  **Choose what you want to order** including pizza size and toppings.

2  **Call the restaurant** and tell the cashier that you have an order for delivery.

3  **Tell the cashier your name, address, and order.**

4  **Ask the cashier how much the pizza will cost** and when it will be delivered.

5  **Count your money** for the pizza and a tip.

6  **Pay and tip the delivery person** when he or she arrives.

#BK-376 Functional Sequencing • ©2010 Super Duper® Publications • www.superduperinc.com • 1-800-277-8737

Pizza Delivery

Vocabulary

pizza	delivery	dough	cost	name
toppings	size	phone	address	count

Conversation Questions

1. What's your favorite pizza topping?

   _____

2. Why does the delivery person need to know your name and address?

   _____

3. When does your family order pizza?

   _____

4. What should you do if the cashier asks to put you on hold?

   _____

5. What should you do if your order is wrong once it is delivered?

   _____

6. What else can you order at a pizza delivery restaurant?

   _____

Extension Activities

1. Ask students why it is okay to tell the person at the pizza delivery place their names and addresses. Ask students to make a list of people whom they should not give their name and address to and why.

2. Put together a pizza-making station with paper cutouts of food (dough, sauce, cheese, pepperoni, etc.). Have students tell you the order in which they put it together.

3. Put students in pairs. Have one student order a pizza while the other one works at the restaurant. Have students practice counting the cost of the pizza and tip with play money.

Ice Cream Parlor

Ice Cream Parlor Name: _____

Address: _____

Phone Number: _____

1  **Look at the menu and choose a flavor of ice cream.**

2  **Wait in line** for the cashier.

3  **Tell the cashier what flavor you want.** The cashier will tell you how much it will cost.

4  **Pay for your ice cream.**

5  Find a place to sit and **eat your ice cream**.

6  **Throw your trash away** when you finish eating.

#BK-376 Functional Sequencing • ©2010 Super Duper® Publications • www.superduperinc.com • 1-800-277-8737

Ice Cream Parlor

Vocabulary

flavor	ice cream	cashier	trash	wait
toppings	order	finish	pay	choose

Conversation Questions

1. What's your favorite flavor of ice cream?

   _____

2. Which toppings do you like on your ice cream?

   _____

3. Why is it important to throw your trash away?

   _____

4. How should you act while waiting in line?

   _____

5. What should you do if your order is wrong?

   _____

6. Where else can you get ice cream besides an ice cream parlor?

   _____

Extension Activities

1. Have students pretend they are in an ice cream shop. Have one student be the ice cream server; another be the cashier; another be the customer. Let them switch roles and say what's different about each role.

2. Ask students what the main ingredient of dairy products is. Ask students to name other dairy products and discuss how they are made.

3. Discuss the differences between ice cream, frozen yogurt, sorbet, sherbert, etc. Help students to research which one is the healthiest and why.

Picnic

A picnic is a fun way to spend time with friends and family. When you go on a picnic, bring foods like sandwiches, fruit, crackers, and cookies. Make sure you check the weather before you leave!

1  **Pack a picnic basket** with foods you like to eat.

2  **Go to a park or field** where you can have a picnic.

3  **Set your food out** on a picnic table or tablecloth.

4  **Eat your food.**

5  **Throw your trash away** when you finish eating.

6  **Pack up everything you brought.** Do not leave anything behind.

Picnic

Vocabulary

sandwich	tablecloth	park	invite	picnic
basket	field	weather	recycle	safety

Conversation Questions

1. Why should you check the weather before going on a picnic?

   _____

2. Who would you like to invite on a picnic and why?

   _____

3. Why do you need to pack up everything you brought to the picnic?

   _____

4. What kinds of foods would not be good for a picnic?

   _____

5. What are some safety rules to follow while you are in a park?

   _____

6. Where else can you go on a picnic besides a park or field?

   _____

Extension Activities

1. Have students bring their lunches to school and have a picnic outside on the school's playground. If the weather doesn't permit an outside picnic, lay out a blanket on your classroom floor and picnic inside!

2. Discuss recycling with students. Ask them what items at a picnic can be recycled.

3. Ask students to draw items in a picnic basket. Look at each drawing and discuss how each thing in the basket is affected by where it was put. For example, if the student put drinks on top of a sandwich, the sandwich may get smashed.

Hygiene

Washing Your Hands

Washing your hands helps to prevent the spread of germs and illnesses. Use plenty of soap and scrub your hands for at least 20 seconds. You can hum a song like "Happy Birthday" or "ABCs" to help you keep track of time.

1  Turn on warm water from the faucet and **wet your hands**.

2  **Put soap on your hands.** Pump soap from a bottle or rub a bar of soap between your hands.

3  **Rub your hands together** for at least 20 seconds. Scrub between your fingers too.

4  **Rinse your hands** under the water until all of the soap is gone.

5 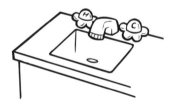 **Turn off the water faucet.**

6  **Dry your hands** with a clean towel.

#BK-376 Functional Sequencing • ©2010 Super Duper® Publications • www.superduperinc.com • 1-800-277-8737

Washing Your Hands

Vocabulary

germs	soap	dry	clean	faucet
warm	seconds	illness	towel	hot

Conversation Questions

1. Why is it important to wash your hands?

   _____

2. When should you wash your hands?

   _____

3. Why do you need to make sure you rinse all the soap off your hands?

   _____

4. What should you do if the faucet drips after you turn off the water?

   _____

5. How many seconds should you wash your hands?

   _____

6. What should you do if the water is too hot?

   _____

Extension Activities

1. Make a chart with each student's name on it. Give students stickers next to their names every time they wash their hands.

2. Ask students to draw pictures of clocks. Then, have them show you all of the times of day they should wash their hands.

3. Sometimes a sink is not always available to wash your hands. Discuss with students other alternatives to soap and water that help keep hands clean. Bring in examples (wipes, hand sanitizer, etc.).

Brushing Your Teeth

Brushing your teeth helps prevent cavities, keeps your gums healthy, and freshens your breath. Brush your teeth for 2 minutes after every meal. Do not leave the water running while you brush your teeth. Turn on the water only as you need it.

1  Turn on water from the faucet and **wet your toothbrush**.

2  Remove the cap on the toothpaste. **Squeeze toothpaste onto your toothbrush,** about the size of a pea.

3  **Rub the bristles on all sides of your teeth** in small circles. Brush your gums and tongue too.

4  **Spit in the sink** and rinse your toothbrush well.

5  **Rinse your mouth** with water and spit again.

6  Put the cap back on the toothpaste and **put away your toothbrush**.

#BK-376 Functional Sequencing • ©2010 Super Duper® Publications • www.superduperinc.com • 1-800-277-8737

Brushing Your Teeth

Vocabulary

toothbrush	cavities	toothpaste	bristles	gums
water	brush	spit	teeth	tongue

Conversation Questions

1. Why should you brush your teeth?

   _____

2. Which type of doctor takes care of teeth?

   _____

3. What should you do if one of your teeth starts hurting?

   _____

4. Why shouldn't you swallow toothpaste?

   _____

5. What should you do after you brush your teeth?

   _____

6. If you wear braces, do you brush your teeth differently?

   _____

Extension Activities

1. Ask students to practice brushing the teeth on a fake mouth like a Mighty Mouth® or Chattering Teeth. Discuss different brushing techniques.

2. Discuss with students the benefits of water conservation. Research how much water is wasted by leaving faucet on while brushing your teeth. Calculate how many gallons a week, month, or year the entire class could save by turning off the faucet while they brush.

3. Ask students to make a list of other things they need to do to keep their teeth healthy.

Getting Dressed

Spring Weather: pants, t-shirt, and a light jacket
Summer Weather: shorts or skirt and t-shirt
Fall Weather: pants, sweatshirt, and a jacket
Winter Weather: pants, sweater, coat, hat, and mittens

Hygiene

1  **Take off your pajamas or dirty clothes.**

2  **Put on clean underwear.**
If you are a girl, put on a bra.

3  **Put on your shirt.**

4  **Pull on your pants, shorts, or skirt.**

5  **Pull on your socks.**

6  **Put on your shoes.**

#BK-376 Functional Sequencing • ©2010 Super Duper® Publications • www.superduperinc.com • 1-800-277-8737

Getting Dressed

Vocabulary

pajamas	shirt	shoes	jacket	wait
underwear	socks	pants	weather	choose

Conversation Questions

1. Why do you wear different clothes depending on the season?

   _____

2. Why is it important to put on clean underwear each day?

   _____

3. What clothes would you choose to wear on a hot, summer day?

   _____

4. What kinds of shoes can you wear without socks?

   _____

5. What clothes would you choose to wear on a cold, winter day?

   _____

6. What is your favorite outfit to wear?

   _____

Extension Activities

1. Some places in the world don't have all four seasons, so the people there don't follow the same weather rules for dressing. Ask students to point out places on a world map that don't have all four seasons.

2. Ask students to cut out different pieces of clothing from a magazine or newspaper. Then, ask them to dress a person they draw with the clothes for each of the different seasons.

3. Have a jacket drive at school. Ask students to bring in old coats to donate to charity.

Wearing Deodorant

Wearing deodorant helps you smell fresh and helps prevent sweating. Remember to put deodorant on every day, especially if you will be doing things that make you sweat a lot, like sports.

1  **Take the cap off** the deodorant.

2  **Turn the dial** at the bottom of the deodorant to make more come out.

3  **Rub the deodorant across one underarm** three or four times.

4  **Rub the deodorant across the other underarm** three or four times.

5  **Put the cap on** the deodorant.

6 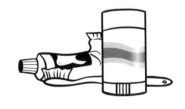 **Put the deodorant away.**

#BK-376 Functional Sequencing • ©2010 Super Duper® Publications • www.superduperinc.com • 1-800-277-8737

Wearing Deodorant

Vocabulary

deodorant	dial	cap	share	choice
underarm	sweat	rub	scent	consistency

Conversation Questions

1. What does deodorant do?

   _____

2. When should you put on deodorant?

   _____

3. How do you know when you are supposed to start wearing deodorant?

   _____

4. Is it okay to share deodorant?

   _____

5. Why might you want to wear a clear deodorant instead of white?

   _____

6. What should you put on first, deodorant or your shirt and why?

   _____

Extension Activities

1. Deodorant comes in different smells, shapes, and consistencies. Ask students to list reasons why there might be so many choices.

2. Ask students to draw five other things that have scents.

3. Ask students to list types of stores where deodorant is sold. Ask them to name two other things they can buy at each of the stores.

Taking a Bath

Keeping your body clean is very important. Bathing every day will make you smell good and feel fresh.

1  **Turn on warm water in the tub.** Close the drain or put the plug in the drain to keep the water in.

2  Take off your clothes. **Carefully step into the tub and sit down.**

3  **Wet and wash your hair** with shampoo. **Rinse your hair** with water.

4  **Wash your body** with soap and a wash cloth. **Rinse your body** with water.

5  **Carefully step out of the tub. Dry off** with a towel.

6  Open the drain or pull the plug out of the drain to **let the water out.**

#BK-376 Functional Sequencing • ©2010 Super Duper® Publications • www.superduperinc.com • 1-800-277-8737

Taking a Bath

Vocabulary

drain	bath	dry	rinse	hair
tub	shampoo	towel	soap	bathe

Conversation Questions

1. Why should you use a washcloth?

   _____

2. Why do you need to be really careful getting in and out of the tub?

   _____

3. Where should you hang your towel after you dry off?

   _____

4. What should you do if you get shampoo in your eyes?

   _____

5. What should you do if you need to go to the bathroom while you are in the tub?

   _____

6. Why is it important to bathe every day?

   _____

Extension Activities

1. Give students towels and have them practice drying off.

2. Bring in a rubber baby doll and let students take turns washing the baby.

3. Everything that goes down the drain goes into a water system, whether you have a septic or sewer system. For this reason, you cannot dump chemicals that will hurt the environment down the drain. Ask students to brainstorm lists of things that cannot go down a drain (bathtub or sink).

Taking a Shower

Keeping your body clean is very important. Showering everyday will make you smell good and feel fresh.

1  **Turn on warm water in the shower.** Turn on the shower head.

2  Take off your clothes. **Carefully step into the shower.**

3  **Wet and wash your hair** with shampoo. **Rinse your hair** with water.

4  **Wash your body** with soap and a washcloth. **Rinse your body** with water.

5  **Turn off the water** when you finish.

6  **Carefully step out of the shower. Dry off** with a towel.

#BK-376 Functional Sequencing • ©2010 Super Duper® Publications • www.superduperinc.com • 1-800-277-8737

Taking a Shower

Vocabulary

wash	dry	shampoo	shower	clean
cold	hot	messy	clothes	conservation

Conversation Questions

1. What should you do if the water is too hot or too cold?

   _____

2. Why do you need to make sure you rinse all of the shampoo and soap off of you?

   _____

3. How do you tell the difference between the hot water and cold water knobs in your tub or shower?

   _____

4. Why do you need to take your clothes off to take a shower?

   _____

5. Which do you prefer, a bath or a shower?

   _____

6. When should you take a shower?

   _____

Extension Activities

1. Ask students whether they think a bath or a shower uses more water. Discuss why water conservation is important.

2. Ask students to draw a clean bathroom and a messy bathroom. Ask them to describe the differences.

3. Ask students to list all of the different products they use in the shower (shampoo, conditioner, body wash, etc.) and what each one is for.

Washing Your Hair

Shampoo cleans dirt and oil from your hair. Conditioner makes your hair soft and easier to comb. You only need to use a small amount of shampoo and conditioner, about the size of a dime.

Hygiene

1  While you are in the bath or shower, **wet your hair**.

2  **Squeeze a small amount of shampoo into your hand.**

3  **Rub the shampoo through your hair.** Close your eyes to keep the bubbles out.

4  **Rinse your hair** under the water until the shampoo is gone.

5  **If you use conditioner, squeeze a small amount into your hand. Rub it through your hair.**

6  **Rinse your hair** under the water until the conditioner is gone.

#BK-376 Functional Sequencing • ©2010 Super Duper® Publications • www.superduperinc.com • 1-800-277-8737

Washing Your Hair

Vocabulary

conditioner	hair	wash	squeeze	bubbles
shampoo	eyes	rinse	bath	comb

Conversation Questions

1. Why would you use conditioner?

   _____

2. What should you do if you use the last bit of shampoo?

   _____

3. Why should you close your eyes while shampoo is in your hair?

   _____

4. How do you know when all the shampoo is out of your hair?

   _____

5. How do you know when to wash your hair?

   _____

6. Where do you keep shampoo and conditioner?

   _____

Extension Activities

1. Ask students why some people might use more shampoo than others.

2. Discuss differences in washing your hair in the bath versus the shower.

3. Ask students to name three other things besides shampoo that make bubbles.

Shaving Your Face

Facial hair is a normal part of growing up. Some people have lots of facial hair and can grow full beards and mustaches. Some people don't have as much facial hair.

1  **Put a small amount of shaving cream into your hand,** about the size of a quarter.

2  **Spread the shaving cream around your face where facial hair grows—** your chin, jaw line, upper lip, and neck.

3  **Use the sharp razor edge to shave off the hair and cream.**

4  **Rinse the razor** with water after each stroke.

5  **Shave and rinse until all of the hair and cream is gone.**

6  **Rinse your face and razor.** Put your razor away.

#BK-376 Functional Sequencing • ©2010 Super Duper® Publications • www.superduperinc.com • 1-800-277-8737

Shaving Your Face

Hygiene

Vocabulary

facial hair	razor	chin	stroke	cultural
shaving cream	lips	shave	neck	beard

Conversation Questions

1. Why do you use shaving cream?

   _____

2. Why do you rinse the razor?

   _____

3. Where do you keep your shaving cream and razor?

   _____

4. What happens if you use too much shaving cream? Not enough?

   _____

5. What should you do after you rinse your face?

   _____

6. What should you shave your face in front of?

   _____

Extension Activities

1. Ask students why some people shave their faces. Discuss cultural/religious reasons also.

2. Bring in shaving cream and spray it on a table. Let students draw in it with their fingers.

3. Have students look through magazines and cut out pictures of men. Sort the pictures into different categories (beard, mustache, goatee, no facial hair, etc.) and calculate which is the most common and least common.

Shaving Your Legs

People shave their legs for different reasons. Some people do it for looks, others for sports.

1 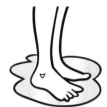 While you are in the bath or shower, **wet your legs**.

2  **Put a small amount of shaving cream into your hand,** about the size of a quarter.

3  **Spread the shaving cream all over your legs.**

4  **Use the sharp razor edge to shave off the hair and cream.**

5  **Rinse the razor** with water after each stroke.

6  **Shave and rinse until all of the hair and cream is gone.**

#BK-376 Functional Sequencing • ©2010 Super Duper® Publications • www.superduperinc.com • 1-800-277-8737

Shaving Your Legs

Vocabulary

legs	razor	rinse	shower	body
blade	shave	bath	share	help

Conversation Questions

1. Why do you use shaving cream?

   _____

2. Why does the razor need to be sharp?

   _____

3. What should you do if you cut yourself shaving?

   _____

4. Why do people shave their legs?

   _____

5. What should you do before you put shaving cream on your legs?

   _____

6. How do you know when you've rinsed your legs well enough?

   _____

Extension Activities

1. If it is your first time shaving, why might you ask for help? Who would you ask?

2. Ask students why they shouldn't share razors. Discuss types of things it is okay to share with others and things that aren't.

3. Give students flyers for local drugstores. Ask them to compare the price and features of the razors to find the best deal.

Shaving Your Underarms

People shave their underarms for different reasons. Some people do it for looks, hygiene reasons, and others for sports.

1  While you are in the bath or shower, **wet your underarms**.

2  **Put a small amount of shaving cream into your hand,** about the size of a dime.

3  **Spread the shaving cream all over your underarms.**

4  **Use the sharp razor edge to shave off the hair and cream.**

5  **Rinse the razor** with water after each stroke.

6  **Shave and rinse until all of the hair and cream is gone.**

#BK-376 Functional Sequencing • ©2010 Super Duper® Publications • www.superduperinc.com • 1-800-277-8737

Shaving Your Underarms

Vocabulary

underarms	razor	shaving cream	safety	sharp
shave	hair	rinse	dull	puberty

Conversation Questions

1. Why do people shave their underarms?

   _____

2. What should you do after wetting your underarms, but before shaving?

   _____

3. What happens if you don't rinse off all of the shaving cream?

   _____

4. Should you use someone else's razor to shave your underarms?

   _____

5. When should you shave your underarms?

   _____

6. Why should you use shaving cream?

   _____

Extension Activities

1. Have students use the internet to research different kinds of razors and their features.

2. Ask students to discuss safety rules about shaving.

3. Cover a balloon in shaving cream. Have the students practice shaving the balloon while noticing pressure and direction of each stroke.

Household Chores

Changing Your Bedding

Put clean sheets, pillowcases, and blankets on your bed at least once a week.

1  **Take the dirty sheets, pillowcases, and blankets off of the bed.** Get clean bedding.

2 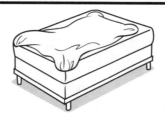 **Lay the clean fitted (elastic) sheet on the mattress.** The short ends go at the head and the foot of the bed.

3  **Pull each corner of the sheet over each corner of the mattress.**

4  **Put the pillowcase on the pillow;** then put and the pillow at the head of the bed.

5  **Lay the clean top sheet on the bed.**

6  **Lay the clean blanket on the bed.**

#BK-376 Functional Sequencing • ©2010 Super Duper® Publications • www.superduperinc.com • 1-800-277-8737

Changing Your Bedding

Vocabulary

mattress	sheets	blanket	bed	dirty
pillowcase	bedding	fitted sheet	clean	elastic

Conversation Questions

1. How often should you change your bedding?

   _____

2. Do you have a favorite blanket or pillow? Tell me about it.

   _____

3. How do you know which way to put the sheets on the bed?

   _____

4. Why should you change your bedding?

   _____

5. Do you put a blanket on the bed first or the fitted sheet?

   _____

6. What should you do with the dirty sheets?

   _____

Extension Activities

1. Depending on where you live, you may use different bedding during different seasons. Discuss this with students and why. Consider things such as using quilts and flannel sheets when the weather is really cold.

2. Give students pieces of construction paper labeled "mattress," "fitted sheet," "sheet," and "blanket." Ask students to "make the bed" in the correct sequence.

3. Ask students to discuss the differences between a twin, full, queen, and king-size bed.

Taking Out the Trash

Trash can make your house smell bad. When the trash can is full, it is time to empty it.

1  **Take the lid off** of the trash can.

2  **Tie a knot at the top of the trash bag** to close it shut.

3  **Pull the trash bag out** of the trash can.

4  **Take the full trash bag outside** to the trash container.

5 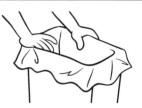 **Put a new trash bag in** the trash can. Stretch the top of the bag around the outside of the trash can.

6  **Put the lid on** the trash can.

Taking Out the Trash

Vocabulary

trash	empty	cardboard	landfill	chemicals
full	glass	bag	recycle	plastic

Conversation Questions

1. How do you know when to take the trash out?

   _____

2. Which do you do first, put the new trash bag in the trash can or tie a knot in the full one?

   _____

3. Why do you need to take the trash out?

   _____

4. What should you do with the full bag of trash?

   _____

5. Are there different kinds of trash bags?

   _____

6. Should you throw cardboard, glass, or plastic away? Why or why not?

   _____

Extension Activities

1. Ask students to draw what they think happens to trash after it leaves their houses. Then, discuss landfills with students.

2. Ask students to write their own sequence of steps for emptying the recycling container. They can use "Taking Out the Trash" for the basis.

3. Everything that gets thrown out ends up in the environment. Ask students to brainstorm lists of things that cannot be thrown away in a regular trash can because they will hurt the environment.

Mopping the Floor

Mopping floors like in your kitchen and bathroom helps keep them clean. Be careful not to slip on the wet floor while you are mopping! You should sweep the floor to remove loose dirt before you begin to mop.

1  **Pour a small amount of floor cleaner into a bucket,** about the size of a quarter.

2  **Fill the bucket with warm water.**

3  **Dip the mop into the bucket** and squeeze out the extra water.

4  **Push the mop back and forth across the floor.** Mop a small section at a time.

5  **Dip the mop into the bucket to rinse** and squeeze out the extra water.

6 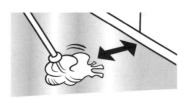 **Repeat steps 4 and 5** until the entire floor is clean.

#BK-376 Functional Sequencing • ©2010 Super Duper® Publications • www.superduperinc.com • 1-800-277-8737

Mopping the Floor

Vocabulary

mopping	mop	squeeze	extra	push
bucket	clean	cleaner	dip	section

Conversation Questions

1. Why should you mop the floor?

   _____

2. What do you need to be careful of after you mop?

   _____

3. What should you do with the mop and bucket after you finish mopping?

   _____

4. What should you do before you mop?

   _____

5. What should you do if the mop water gets really dirty?

   _____

6. Do you mop hardwood floors or carpet?

   _____

Extension Activities

1. Give students different kinds of mops (flop-top, sponge, Swiffer®) and ask them to tell you how they would mop differently using the different mops.

2. Ask students to draw their own sequences for cleaning the floor from picking up, to sweeping/vacuuming, to mopping.

3. Many times when someone mops a floor at school or in a store, they will place a caution sign near the mopped area. Discuss with students other signs that warn people of things.

Vacuuming the Carpet

Vacuuming regularly keeps carpets clean. The vacuum sucks up dirt from the carpet and catches it in a bag or canister.

1  **Plug in the vacuum and turn it on.**

2  **Press the button that releases the handle** so that the vacuum leans back.

3  **Push the vacuum back and forth across the carpet.**

4  **Use the vacuum hose to clean under furniture** and in small places.

5  **Turn the vacuum off and unplug it.**

6  **Empty the dirt canister or change the bag** when it is full.

#BK-376 Functional Sequencing • ©2010 Super Duper® Publications • www.superduperinc.com • 1-800-277-8737

Vacuuming the Carpet

Vocabulary

vacuum	plug	clean	empty	dirt canister
button	handle	unplug	bag	carpet

Conversation Questions

1. **Why should you vacuum?**

   _____

2. **When do you use the vacuum hose instead of the vacuum?**

   _____

3. **What happens if you don't empty the dirt canister or change the bag?**

   _____

4. **How do you turn on the vacuum?**

   _____

5. **What happens if you don't release the vacuum handle?**

   _____

6. **What should you do with the vacuum when you finish cleaning?**

   _____

Extension Activities

1. Ask students to name three safety rules to follow when using the vacuum.

2. Some vacuums have additional settings such as pile height and floor type. Discuss with students when they should adjust the settings.

3. Give students 15 seconds to list as many things as they can that should not be vacuumed. The student who lists the most wins!

Dusting the Furniture

Dusting regularly keeps furniture clean. Dusting also keeps the air in your house clean. Dust using furniture polish on hard surfaces like tables, shelves, and dressers. Do not use furniture polish on cushions, TVs, or stereos.

1  **Get an old cloth and furniture polish** to dust the furniture.

2  **Spray a thin layer of polish on a piece of furniture.**

3  **Use the cloth to wipe off the polish and dust.**

4  **Spray a thin layer of polish on another piece of furniture.**

5  **Use the cloth to wipe off the polish and dust.**

6  **Repeat steps 4 and 5** until all of the hard surfaces in your house are clean.

#BK-376 Functional Sequencing • ©2010 Super Duper® Publications • www.superduperinc.com • 1-800-277-8737

Dusting the Furniture

Vocabulary

dusting	cloth	furniture	spray	thin
polish	wipe	electronics	surfaces	layer

Conversation Questions

1. What does dusting do?

   _____

2. What kinds of furniture should you not use furniture polish on?

   _____

3. How do you know if you are using too much or too little furniture polish?

   _____

4. How do you know when to dust?

   _____

5. What can you use to wipe off electronics?

   _____

6. Why do you need to use an old cloth?

   _____

Extension Activities

1. Give students cloths and furniture polish and have them practice dusting.

2. When using chemicals, students need to follow safety instructions such as aiming spray away from their bodies, not breathing in fumes, etc. Review safety rules with students.

3. Dust is made up of lots of particles. Have students brainstorm as many things as they can that help to make dust.

Hand-Washing Dishes

Dirty dishes can attract bugs and germs. Keep your kitchen clean and yourself healthy by washing dirty dishes every day. Before washing plates and bowls, scrape large pieces of food into the trash can.

1  **Turn on warm water in the sink.**

2  **Add a squirt of dish soap** to the running water.

3  **Place dirty plates, utensils, and glasses in the sink.**

4  **Scrub each plate, utensil, and glass** with a dishcloth or sponge to remove all of the food.

5  **Rinse the dishes** with clean water.

6  **Set the dishes on a dish rack** to dry.

#BK-376 Functional Sequencing • ©2010 Super Duper® Publications • www.superduperinc.com • 1-800-277-8737

Hand-Washing Dishes

Vocabulary

dish soap	dishes	scrape	rinse	utensil
hand-wash	scrub	dishcloth	sponge	dry

Conversation Questions

1. **Why should you wash dishes?**

   _____

2. **Why should you use warm water to wash dishes?**

   _____

3. **Why should you wash dishes in a sink and not a bathtub?**

   _____

4. **What is the difference between a dishcloth and a sponge?**

   _____

5. **What can you use to dry dishes if you don't have a dish rack?**

   _____

6. **Why should you scrape large pieces of food off of plates before washing them?**

   _____

Extension Activities

1. Ask students to make a list of the chores that they can do at home.

2. Chores are always more fun when people help each other. Ask students to help each other pretend to wash dishes by hand, one person can wash, another dry, another put away, etc.

3. Ask students to draw their kitchens and show where the plates, cups, silverware, etc. belong.

Loading the Dishwasher

Using the dishwasher has many steps. After the dishwasher is fully loaded, follow the steps in "Running the Dishwasher" on page 60.

1  **Open the dishwasher door** and pull out the racks.

2  **Put glasses upside down on the top rack.**

3 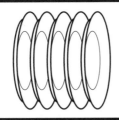 **Put plates standing-up on the bottom rack.** One plate goes in each slot.

4  **Put bowls upside down on the top or the bottom rack.**

5 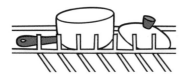 **Put pots, pans, and other large dishes upside down on the bottom rack.**

6  **Put silverware in the basket.** Spoons and forks go in with handles down. Knives go in with handles up.

#BK-376 Functional Sequencing • ©2010 Super Duper® Publications • www.superduperinc.com • 1-800-277-8737

Loading the Dishwasher

Vocabulary

rinse	dishwasher	upside down	plates	loaded
water	glasses	silverware	pots	rack

Conversation Questions

1. Where is the dishwasher located?

   _____

2. Why are bowls placed upside down?

   _____

3. What kinds of things cannot be washed in the dishwasher?

   _____

4. How do you know when the dishwasher is full?

   _____

5. Why are knives placed with their handles up?

   _____

6. What should you do when the dishwasher is fully loaded?

   _____

Extension Activities

1. Ask students to draw a dishwasher and label where different items belong.

2. Sometimes dishes break while in the dishwasher. Discuss with students how they should clean up a broken dish.

3. Some items won't fit in a dishwasher. Ask students to come up with their own sequences as to what they should do with those dishes.

Running the Dishwasher

After you fully load the dishwasher, it's time to run it! Remember only use dishwasher detergent in the dishwasher. Never open the door to the dishwasher while it is running—the water is very hot!

1  **Open the dishwasher door.**

2  **Pour dishwasher detergent into both dishwasher cups.** If there are covers on the cups, close them.

3 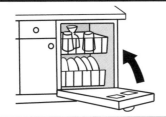 **Close the dishwasher door.**

4 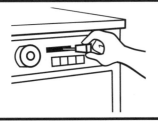 **Pull the lever** to lock the dishwasher door.

5  **Choose a cleaning cycle and press the start button.**

6  When the dishwasher finishes its cleaning cycle, **open the door and put the dishes away**.

#BK-376 Functional Sequencing • ©2010 Super Duper® Publications • www.superduperinc.com • 1-800-277-8737

Household Chores

Running the Dishwasher

Vocabulary

dishwasher	detergent	button	lever	finish
cleaning cycle	dishes	door	start	cover

Conversation Questions

1. **When is the dishwasher ready to run?**

   _____

2. **Why shouldn't you open the dishwasher while it is running?**

   _____

3. **What should you do when the dishwasher finishes running?**

   _____

4. **What are the different cleaning cycles to choose from?**

   _____

5. **Why do you need to put dishes away after the dishwasher is finished?**

   _____

6. **Why should you only use dishwasher detergent in the dishwasher and not any other detergents?**

   _____

Extension Activities

1. Make a cleaning cycle dial with paper attached to cardboard with a brad. Show students pictures of dishes and have them set the cycle based on how dirty the dishes are.

2. Put students into pairs and ask the pairs to come up with the sequence of the dishwasher cleaning dishes. The pair that is correct wins!

3. Sometimes dishes aren't thoroughly clean when they come out of the dishwasher. Discuss with students what they should do if they don't think the dishes are clean after running the dishwasher.

Using the Washing Machine

Before washing your laundry, sort it into different piles.
White laundry gets washed with hot water.
Light-colored laundry gets washed with warm water.
Dark-colored laundry gets washed with cold water.

1 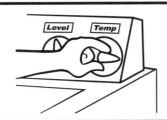 **Turn the temperature dial to the correct setting** for the color of laundry you are washing.

2 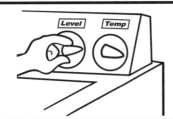 **Turn the size dial to the correct setting** for the amount of laundry you are washing.

3  **Open the lid and pour laundry detergent into the washing machine.** Check the back of the detergent box or bottle to see how much to add.

4  **Put the laundry into the washing machine.** Spread it around the inside evenly.

5  **Close the lid and pull the knob** to start the washing machine.

6  When the washing machine finishes its cleaning cycle, **take out the laundry**.

#BK-376 Functional Sequencing • ©2010 Super Duper® Publications • www.superduperinc.com • 1-800-277-8737

Vocabulary

lights	laundry	warm	detergent	knob
darks	hot	cold	temperature	lid

Conversation Questions

1. Why should you wash clothes?

   _____

2. How do you know how much detergent to use?

   _____

3. What temperature water should you use for lights? Darks?

   _____

4. How do you know which size setting to use on the washing machine?

   _____

5. Why do you need to close the lid to the washing machine before the wash cycle begins?

   _____

6. Why should you sort your laundry before you wash it?

   _____

Extension Activities

1. Cut out pictures of clothing from magazines. Ask students to sort the pictures into different color laundry piles to wash.

2. Ask students to list different wash cycles and the types of clothes that get washed in them.

3. Discuss what might happen if too much detergent is used for a wash cycle, and why using the correct amount is important.

Using the Dryer

After you wash your laundry in the washing machine, you can put it in the dryer. Check the tags on clothes to see if they can go in the dryer. Some clothes like sweaters may shrink in the dryer, and have to air-dry instead.

1 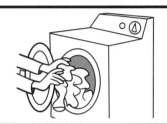 **Open the door and put the laundry into the dryer.**

2  **Put a dryer sheet into the dryer and close the door.**

3  **Turn the dial to the correct temperature and time setting** for the type of laundry you are drying.

4 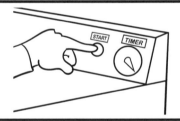 **Turn or press the "Start" button** to turn on the dryer.

5  When the dryer finishes its drying cycle, **check to see if the laundry is dry**.

6  If your laundry is not dry, turn on the dryer again. When the dryer finishes its drying cycle, **take out the laundry**.

#BK-376 Functional Sequencing • ©2010 Super Duper® Publications • www.superduperinc.com • 1-800-277-8737

Using the Dryer

Vocabulary

dryer	dial	fold	shrink	press
setting	damp	air-dry	turn	dryer sheet

Conversation Questions

1. What do you use the dryer for?

   _____

2. What do you put into the dryer with your laundry?

   _____

3. What types of clothing may shrink in the dryer?

   _____

4. What should you do if your laundry is still damp when the dryer stops?

   _____

5. Why do you need to close the door to the dryer?

   _____

6. What should you do with your laundry once it is dry?

   _____

Extension Activities

1. Discuss types of clothing that do not get dried in the dryer. Bring in "laundry" for students to sort into piles of what gets put in the dryer or not.

2. Discuss why you might hang clothes on a clothes line instead of drying clothes in a dryer. Have students list pros and cons of each.

3. Hold up different types of clothing. Ask students which dryer setting they would use to dry the item. Discuss why.

Safety

911 Emergency

911

Dialing 911 is for serious emergencies only. Some examples of a serious emergency are: a house on fire; a car accident where people are injured; someone cannot breathe or cannot wake up; someone is in terrible pain from an injury or illness.

1  If you witness or have a serious emergency, **find a safe place to use the phone**.

2  **Stay calm and dial 911.**

3  **Tell the operator your name and location.**

4  **Tell the operator what has happened.**

5 **Listen carefully and follow the directions** from the operator.

6  **Do not hang up the phone** until the operator says to do so.

#BK-376 Functional Sequencing • ©2010 Super Duper® Publications • www.superduperinc.com • 1-800-277-8737

911 Emergency

Vocabulary

phone	operator	listen	emergency	accident
injury	pain	911	address	directions

Conversation Questions

1. What is an emergency?

   _____

2. What number do you call if you have a serious emergency and need help?

   _____

3. Who answers your 911 calls?

   _____

4. What do you tell the operator when you call 911?

   _____

5. What should you do while the operator is speaking to you?

   _____

6. When do you hang up the phone?

   _____

Extension Activities

1. Ask two students to pretend there is an emergency. Have them play the roles of the caller and the 911 operator. Students can use the sequence on page 80 as a prompt.

2. Ask students to make a list of emergencies that require calling 911 and those that do not need 911 assistance.

3. Ask students to discuss why calling 911 for non-emergencies is unnecessary and illegal. Explain that calling 911 in a non-emergency situation keeps the operator from answering calls that are serious. Emphasize that dialing 911 as a joke or a prank is a crime.

Police Department

Call the Police Department for non-emergency situations. Some examples of when to call the police are: a car accident where no one is injured or something has been stolen from you.

1  If you witness or have a non-emergency situation, **find a safe place to use the phone**.

2  **Stay calm and call the police** for help. **Dial** _____.

3  **Tell the operator your name and location.**

4  **Tell the operator what has happened.**

5 **Listen carefully and follow the directions** from the operator.

6  **Do not hang up the phone** until the operator says to do so.

Police Department

Vocabulary

police	operator	non-emergency	injured	accident
address	directions	phone number	stolen	assistance

Conversation Questions

1. Why do you call the police department for some situations and not 911?

   _____

2. Why should you tell the operator the phone number and address of where you are?

   _____

3. What should you tell the operator after you give your address and phone number?

   _____

4. What should you do while the operator is speaking to you?

   _____

5. When do you hang up the phone with the operator?

   _____

6. What kind of situations should you report to the police department?

   _____

Extension Activities

1. Make small cards that students can carry with them that have their local police department telephone number on it. Below it list non-emergencies that require calling police (theft, minor car accident). Next, list 911 and emergencies that require calling 911 (fire, injury).

2. Ask a local police officer to come and speak to students about crime and safety.

3. Ask students to listen to a list (prepared by the teacher) of emergencies and non-emergencies. Have students decide if they would call 911, the police, or do nothing and why.

Poison Control

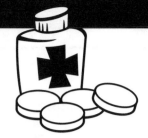

If you (or someone you are with) swallow something that makes you sick, call Poison Control to find out what you should do.

1  **Stay calm and call Poison Control** for help. **Dial** _____.

2  **Tell the operator your name.**

3 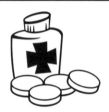 **Tell the operator what you** (or someone you are with) **swallowed and how much.**

4 **Listen carefully** to the operator.

5  **Write down all of the instructions** the operator gives you. Repeat the instructions back to the operator.

6  **If you need help, call someone you trust.**

Poison Control

Vocabulary

medicines	invisible	solids	berries	Quills Up!
liquid	smell	plants	poisons	sprays

Conversation Questions

1. What does it mean when something is "poisonous"?

   _____

2. Who should you call if you swallow something that makes you sick?

   _____

3. What should you tell the poison control or 911 operator?

   _____

4. Why are you not able to tell if some things are poisonous?

   _____

5. Why should you not take medicine without an adult's help or supervision?

   _____

6. Why should you never put anything in your mouth that you are not sure is safe to eat or drink?

   _____

Extension Activities

1. Collect items or pictures of items commonly found around the home and show them to the students. Ask students to decide whether the items are safe or not safe to eat/drink and tell why.

2. Ask students to draw an item that is unsafe to eat/drink. Display the pictures.

3. Contact your local Poison Control for information about Spike and *Quills Up!* Complete the lessons with students.

Answering the Telephone

Never tell someone who calls on the telephone that you are home alone. Do not give personal information to people who call.

1  When you hear the telephone ring, **pick up the receiver and say, "Hello."**

2  If you do not know the person who is calling **ask, "Who is calling, please?"**

3  **If you are home alone say, "My parents are busy right now. May I take a message?"**

4  **Write down the message.**

5  Mrs. Johnson is on the telephone.

If an adult is home say, "Hold on, please." Tell the adult who is on the phone.

6  When you finish talking **say, "Goodbye" and hang up the phone**.

#BK-376 Functional Sequencing • ©2010 Super Duper® Publications • www.superduperinc.com • 1-800-277-8737

Vocabulary

receiver	stranger	caller	polite	answering machine
message	phone	adult	excuse	accurate

Conversation Questions

1. What should you never tell someone on the phone?

   _____

2. What do you ask a caller when you are at home alone?

   _____

3. What should you say when the caller asks for an adult who is at home?

   _____

4. Why might you let an answering machine take calls when you are alone?

   _____

5. What is personal information?

   _____

6. Why is it important to write down a caller's message and information accurately?

   _____

Extension Activities

1. Ask students to role-play being a caller and a call recipient. Teacher gives caller different information to tell the recipient. Recipient must respond to and take down caller's information accurately. Discuss as a class what happened in each scenario.

2. Ask students what personal information is off limits to tell a caller. Such things might include address, time parents get home, where they go to school and what time, etc.

3. Have students practice with a caller that is insistent on getting personal information from the student. Students should know when to hang up after taking a message.

Answering the Front Door

Never open the door when you are home alone, even if it is someone you know. Never tell anyone that you are home alone. Do not give money or personal information to people who come to your door.

1

When you hear the doorbell ring or someone knocking on your front door, **go to the front door**.

2

Do not open the door.
Ask, "Who is it?"

3

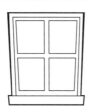

Look out a window or through a peephole to **see if the person is someone you know**.

4

If you are home alone say,
"My parents are busy right now.
Please come back another time."

5

Mrs. Johnson is at the door.

If an adult is home say,
"Hold on, please."
Tell the adult who is at the door.

6

If the person at the door won't
go away, call the police.
Dial_____.

#BK-376 Functional Sequencing • ©2010 Super Duper® Publications • www.superduperinc.com • 1-800-277-8737

Answering the Front Door

Vocabulary

stranger	knock	doorbell	peephole	alone
adult	window	lock	invite	answer

Conversation Questions

1. What should you never tell someone who is knocking at your door?

   _____

2. What should you do when you hear knocking at the door before you ask, "Who is it"?

   _____

3. What should you do when you hear knocking at the door and an adult is home with you?

   _____

4. Why should you never open a door to strangers and invite them inside?

   _____

5. Why should you keep your doors locked when you are home?

   _____

6. Who decides who can come inside your home?

   _____

Extension Activities

1. Ask students to role-play different scenarios of someone at the door. Use scenarios where others are at home and where students are by themselves. Monitor responses and lead discussion.

2. Ask students to list reasons why they should not open the door to strangers even when an adult is home.

3. Ask students to respond to the knocking at the classroom door, pretending it is at their house. Teacher plays the "stranger" who is asking too many questions and being pushy. Students should recognize there may be a point when they should call the police or 911.

Crossing the Street

Crossing the street is an everyday activity, but it can be very dangerous. If you are riding a bike, get off of the bike and walk it across the street.

1 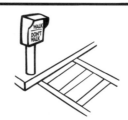 **Go to the nearest crosswalk** to cross the street.

2  **If there is a crossing guard, wait until he or she tells you to cross.**

3   **If there is a crosswalk signal, wait until it says "Walk"** or shows a picture of a person walking.

4   **Stop, look both ways, and listen** for traffic.

5  **If there is no traffic, you may cross the street.**

6  **Never run when crossing the street.** Always walk!

#BK-376 Functional Sequencing • ©2010 Super Duper® Publications • www.superduperinc.com • 1-800-277-8737

Crossing the Street

Vocabulary

traffic light	crosswalk	traffic	crosswalk signal	walk
crossing guard	don't walk	street	dangerous	bike

Conversation Questions

1. Why should you always go to the crosswalk to cross the street?

   _____

2. What does a crossing guard do?

   _____

3. When you are riding your bike, what should you do before you cross the street?

   _____

4. What should you do before crossing a street where there is no crosswalk?

   _____

5. Why do you always walk and never run while crossing the street?

   _____

6. Why is it so dangerous to cross the street when a crossing guard or crossing signal tells you not to cross?

   _____

Extension Activities

1. Ask students to make a list of rules for crossing the street safely at school, on busy streets, and in neighborhoods. Have students draw single illustrations beside each rule. Post pictures in the classroom.

2. Ask a school crossing guard or local police officer to visit the class to discuss street safety.

3. Ask students to role-play crossing the street using crosswalk signals, stop lights, and a crossing guard. Discuss differences with the class.

Staying Safe in a Fire

Wherever you are, you should know what to do in case of a fire. At home, plan a fire escape route with your family. When at public places, always note where the fire exits are when you arrive.

1  **If you smell or see smoke, cover your mouth and nose with a damp towel or shirt** to keep from inhaling dangerous smoke.

2  Smoke rises, so stay low to the ground and **crawl underneath the smoke**.

3  If a door is closed, touch it to see if it is hot. **If the door is hot, do not open it.**

4 FIRE EXIT **Find a way outside.** Follow your family's fire escape route, or look for signs that say "Fire Exit." Do not use an elevator.

5  **Do not stop** to take anything with you or make a phone call for help.

6  **Find a safe place and call 911.**

#BK-376 Functional Sequencing • ©2010 Super Duper® Publications • www.superduperinc.com • 1-800-277-8737

Staying Safe in a Fire

Vocabulary

exit	damp	fire truck	escape route	fire alarm
911	smoke	hot	batteries	safe

Conversation Questions

1. Why is it important for your family to have a fire escape route at home?

   _____

2. What should you do to keep from inhaling dangerous smoke?

   _____

3. Why should you stay low to the ground when trying to escape a fire?

   _____

4. What should you look for in public buildings in case of a fire?

   _____

5. Why should you not use an elevator during a fire?

   _____

6. How do you know not to open certain doors during a fire?

   _____

Extension Activities

1. Ask students to draw a simple floor plan of their homes. Help students develop an escape route and family meeting place. Have students bring the plans home and discuss with their families.

2. Have students study the fire exit plan for their school. Have students practice the fire escape plan and meet you at a designated meeting place while following all fire safety rules.

3. Have students discuss the dangers of taking an elevator, stopping to get personal items, or making a 911 call in an unsafe place during a fire.

CASHIER

Retail Services

Movie and Game Rental Store

Renting movies and games is fun, but it can be expensive if you don't return the items by their due date!

1  Remember to **bring your membership card**.

2  **Find what you want to rent**. Most stores have new releases along the walls and older movies in the center. Ask a salesperson if you need help.

3  **Pick up movies or games** you want to rent.

4  **Wait in line** to pay the cashier.

5  **Give the cashier the movies or games and your membership card.**

6  **Pay the cashier** and take your change, movies or games, and membership card.

#BK-376 Functional Sequencing • ©2010 Super Duper® Publications • www.superduperinc.com • 1-800-277-8737

Movie and Game Rental Store

Vocabulary

membership card	movie	salesperson	return	due date
new release	cashier	movie drop	aisle	late fee

Conversation Questions

1. Why do you think new releases are popular rentals?

_____

2. Why do think most movie and game rental stores display older movies and games in the center aisles?

_____

3. Why might you rent movies and games rather than buy them?

_____

4. Where do you go to pay for your movie and game rentals?

_____

5. Why must you return movies and games by their due date?

_____

6. What is the purpose of having a membership card for movie and game rentals?

_____

Extension Activities

1. Create a mock membership card application. After students fill out the application, go over the application and check information and discuss why it asks for so much personal information.

2. Using old copies of movies, ask three students to role-play (renter, salesperson, cashier) renting a movie. Renter must ask the salesperson for help locating a movie, then present it to the cashier. Cashier checks membership card and collects money. Have students switch roles.

3. Ask students to discuss why they should return movies on time and why stores charge for late returns. Talk about ways to remember return dates in order to avoid late fees.

Retail Services

Movie Rental Kiosk

Renting movies is fun, but it can be expensive if you don't return the items by their due date! Remember, most kiosks only have one-day rentals and will charge you late fees.

1  Remember to **bring your credit or debit card**.

2  **Browse the movies** you can rent by touching the screen.

3  **Select the movie you want** to rent by following the directions on the screen.

4  **Swipe your credit or debit card** to pay for the movie.

5  **Take your movie from the dispenser.** If you rented more than one movie, wait for the next one to dispense.

6  **Remember to return the movie the next day** or you will be charged a late fee!

Movie Rental Kiosk

Vocabulary

kiosk	debit card	credit card	late fee	browse
dispenser	touch screen	due date	decline	swipe

Conversation Questions

1. What does it mean to "browse" the movies for rent?

   _____

2. How is a touch screen different from other computers?

   _____

3. What happens when you swipe a credit or debit card at the kiosk?

   _____

4. What must you do before a movie drops into the dispenser?

   _____

5. Why might you go to a movie rental kiosk instead of a movie rental store?

   _____

6. How do you know the due date to return your movie?

   _____

Extension Activities

1. Sometimes a movie may get jammed in the kiosk. Have students problem solve as to what they should do if this happens. Role-play any responses involving getting help from someone else.

2. Kiosks tend to have newer movies only. Ask students to list ten movies each and then write next to each whether a kiosk is likely to have that movie or not.

3. Credit and debit cards are sometimes declined. Discuss with students what they can do if their credit or debit card is declined at a kiosk.

Shoe Store

Shoes may be sold in a store that only sells shoes, or they may be sold in a store with a shoe department.

1  **Go to the shoe section and look at the type of shoes you need** (athletic shoes, dress shoes, sandals, etc.).

2  If you see shoes you like, **find your size or ask a salesperson for help**.

3 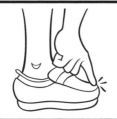 **Try on the shoes to see if they fit properly.** Shoes should be comfortable and not too tight.

4  **Take the shoes you want to buy to the cashier.**

5  **Wait in line** for the cashier.

6  **Pay the cashier** and take your change and your new shoes.

#BK-376 Functional Sequencing • ©2010 Super Duper® Publications • www.superduperinc.com • 1-800-277-8737

Shoe Store

Vocabulary

size	sandals	comfortable	cashier	department
properly	section	fit	tight	change

Conversation Questions

1. Where do you go to buy shoes?

   _____

2. Who can help you find a pair of shoes you like in your size?

   _____

3. How do you know if your shoes fit properly?

   _____

4. What do you do if you find a pair of shoes that you want to buy?

   _____

5. What different types of shoes can you buy?

   _____

6. When can you take your shoes out of the store?

   _____

Extension Activities

1. Ask students to explain what shoes feel like when they fit properly or improperly. Have students try on several different shoes and tell how they fit.

2. Have students discuss the kinds of shoes they wear for different occasions and why those shoes are appropriate. Have students discuss shoes they would not wear for certain occasions and why.

3. Have students draw their favorite pair(s) of shoes and write why they are their favorite shoes.

Clothing Store

Remember, you need different types of clothes for the different seasons. What you buy for summer is different than what you'll buy for winter.

1  **Go to the clothing section and look at the type of clothes you need** (t-shirts, dress clothes, jeans, etc.).

2  If you see clothes you like, **find your size or ask a salesperson for help**.

3  **Try on the clothes in the fitting room.** Clothes should be comfortable and not too tight.

4  Give the clothes you do not want to a salesperson. **Take the clothes you want to buy to the cashier.**

5  **Wait in line** for the cashier.

6  **Pay the cashier** and take your change and your new clothes.

#BK-376 Functional Sequencing • ©2010 Super Duper® Publications • www.superduperinc.com • 1-800-277-8737

Clothing Store

Vocabulary

seasons	size	fitting room	alter	jeans
tailor	hanger	dress shirt	t-shirt	fold

Conversation Questions

1. Why do you wear different types of clothes in different seasons?

   _____

2. Who do you ask to help you find the correct size of clothing you need?

   _____

3. Where do you go to try on the clothes you like?

   _____

4. How should your clothes fit in order to be comfortable?

   _____

5. What do you do with the clothes you want to buy?

   _____

6. What can you do after you pay the cashier for your clothes?

   _____

Extension Activities

1. Ask students to list their favorite places to shop for clothes and why.

2. Discuss what alterations and a tailor are with students. Bring in a bunch of old clothes for students to put on and then say how they would get a tailor to alter them to fit properly.

3. Clothing that does not fit properly can create hazards. Loose, baggy, and clothing that is too long can get caught on things. Discuss different clothing items that can create hazards in everyday life.

Grocery Store

Some people plan meals for the week, some just buy what's on sale—do whichever works for you! Make a list of the groceries you need before you go to the store.

1  **Get a shopping cart or basket.**

2  Start at one side of the grocery store. **Check off items on your list** as you put them into your cart.

3  **Check fresh items like milk, eggs, and bread for an expiration date.** Get the item with the expiration date that is farthest away.

4  **Ask a salesperson if you need help** finding an item.

5  When you finish shopping, **wait in line** for the cashier.

6  **Pay the cashier** and take your change and your food.

#BK-376 Functional Sequencing • ©2010 Super Duper® Publications • www.superduperinc.com • 1-800-277-8737

Grocery Store

Vocabulary

list	expiration date	produce	meat	plan
sale	shopping cart	deli	dairy	aisle

Conversation Questions

1. Why should you make a shopping list before you go to the grocery store?

   _____

2. Why do you need to use a shopping cart or basket?

   _____

3. Why should you check off items on your list as you put them into your cart?

   _____

4. What does the expiration date on food tell you?

   _____

5. Why do people plan their meals before going to the grocery store?

   _____

6. Why do some people only buy items that are on sale at the grocery store?

   _____

Extension Activities

1. Ask students to plan meals for breakfast and dinner for a week. Working in pairs, have students help each other figure out what they need from the grocery store to make the meals and write their lists.

2. Use grocery store flyers to help students learn to budget money. Give each student $100 of play money. Have them figure out meals for a family of four for a week with $100.

3. Ask students to make a list of their 10 favorite foods. Then, have students sort the foods by department (meat, dairy, deli, bakery, produce, etc.).

Hair Salons and Barber Shops

Some hair salons and barber shops require you to make an appointment to get a haircut, and some will take walk-in customers.

1  Look through magazines and **cut out a picture of a hairstyle you like**.

2  **Go to the hair salon or barber shop** at your appointment time or as a walk-in customer.

3  **Show the barber or stylist the picture** of the hairstyle you want.

4  **Sit still** during the haircut.

5  When the barber or stylist finishes, **look at your hair and make sure you like it**.

6  **Pay for your haircut** and tip the barber or stylist.

#BK-376 Functional Sequencing • ©2010 Super Duper® Publications • www.superduperinc.com • 1-800-277-8737

Hair Salons and Barber Shops

Vocabulary

barber	appointment	salon	magazine	style
stylist	walk-in	tip	haircut	still

Conversation Questions

1. Why do many hair salons and barber shops require that you make an appointment?

2. How does having a picture of the hairstyle you want help the barber or stylist?

3. Why should you sit still while the stylist or barber cuts your hair?

4. What is a walk-in customer?

5. Why should you give the stylist or barber a tip?

6. What should you say when the stylist or barber finishes and you like your haircut? What if you don't like your haircut?

Extension Activities

1. Have students role-play being a caller and a stylist or barber. Have the caller make an appointment and then follow the sequence of getting a haircut.

2. Have students discuss and list differences between a stylist and a barber.

3. Take digital pictures of students and print out multiple copies. Have students cut out pictures of hairstyles from magazines and paste them onto their own pictures. Hang the pictures around the room. There are many free computer programs online to use for this activity.

Post Office

When you need to get your mail, buy stamps, or mail a letter or package, go to the post office.

1  **Write the address of where you are sending the letter or package** on its front side.

2  **Go to the post office.**

3  **Wait in line** for the postal worker to help you.

4  **Tell the postal worker what you need.**

5  **Wait quietly** while the postal worker weighs the package for postage or gives you stamps.

6  **Pay the postal worker** and take your change and your stamps.

#BK-376 Functional Sequencing • ©2010 Super Duper® Publications • www.superduperinc.com • 1-800-277-8737

Post Office

Vocabulary

stamps	postal worker	postage	post office	sort
letter	package	weigh	deliver	mail

Conversation Questions

1. Why do you need to buy stamps to mail letters and packages?

   _____

2. Who helps you get what you need at the post office?

   _____

3. Why does the postal worker weigh your package?

   _____

4. Why do you go to the post office?

   _____

5. What do postal workers use to weigh packages and letters?

   _____

6. Why would someone go to the post office to mail a letter instead of letting the postal worker pick it up at their house?

   _____

Extension Activities

1. Ask students to write letters to other people in school. Have students be postal workers and deliver the letters through the school.

2. Have a stamp contest. Give students a sheet of white paper and markers or crayons. Have them design stamps to commemorate special people, occasions, charities, or holidays.

3. Discuss with students all of the things the post office does. Be sure to talk about receiving, sorting, and delivering mail. Free lessons on the history and duties of the U.S. Postal Service can be found online at: www.usps.com/postalhistory.

Bookstore

Bookstores have books grouped by subject. Within each subject, books are sorted by titles or authors' last names.

1  **Go to the section of books you enjoy** (fantasy, non-fiction, cooking, etc.).

2  **Look for the book you want** to buy.

3  If you can't find the book you want, **ask a salesperson for help**.

4  **Take the book you want to buy to the cashier.**

5  **Wait in line** for the cashier.

6  **Pay the cashier** and take your change and your new book.

#BK-376 Functional Sequencing • ©2010 Super Duper® Publications • www.superduperinc.com • 1-800-277-8737

Bookstore

Vocabulary

fiction	fantasy	salesperson	non-fiction	children's
author	title	section	library	bookstore

Conversation Questions

1. What different kinds of books can you find in bookstores?

   _____

2. How do bookstores usually sort books?

   _____

3. Who can help you find a book that you want?

   _____

4. What kinds of books do you like to look at in a bookstore?

   _____

5. What do you do with the books you want to buy?

   _____

6. What else do bookstores sell?

   _____

Extension Activities

1. Write the titles of books from the school library on index cards for students. Each student then has to find the book in the library and write down its author and subject.

2. Put several books on a table and ask students to arrange the books into subjects and by title or author as a bookstore would do.

3. Ask the school librarian to visit the classroom and talk about the ways students can find more information about how to find books in the library or bookstore. Discuss any differences there are between finding books in a library versus a bookstore.

Music Store

Many stores have music sections. Some stores carry only music. Stores divide music into different genres. Within each genre, CDs are sorted by band name or singer's last name.

1  **Go to the section of music you enjoy** (country, jazz, classical, pop, etc.).

2  **Look for the music you want** to buy.

3  If you can't find the music you want, **ask a salesperson for help**.

4  **Take the music you want to buy to the cashier.**

5  **Wait in line** for the cashier.

6  **Pay the cashier** and take your change and your new music.

#BK-376 Functional Sequencing • ©2010 Super Duper® Publications • www.superduperinc.com • 1-800-277-8737

Music Store

Vocabulary

genre	band	CD	salesperson	sort
music	singer	song	download	copy

Conversation Questions

1. How many different styles of music can you name?

   _____

2. Why do some stores allow you to listen to a CD before you buy it?

   _____

3. What other things might a music store sell besides CDs?

   _____

4. How do music stores sort music?

   _____

5. Who can help you if you cannot find the music you want to buy?

   _____

6. What should you do if you don't know the genre a band belongs to?

   _____

Extension Activities

1. Have each student make a list of their favorite songs. Then, as a class, sort everyone's songs into different genres. Turn this list into a graph or pie chart to integrate math skills.

2. Ask students to explain how they would sort music in a music store if they could do it however they wanted. Have them draw a picture of the layout.

3. Discuss with students the pros and cons of listening to a CD in a store, downloading music, making copies of CDs, etc. Discuss legal issues of copying music by referring to the Recording Industry Association of America at: www.riaa.com/physicalpiracy.php.

Online Stores

You can shop online for almost anything. Many stores have websites and some stores are only on the web.

1  Type in the store's web address or use a search engine to **find the store that you want**.

2  **Browse through the store's collection** of items or type in what you are searching for.

3  **Follow the site's directions for how to purchase items.** If you need help, visit the Help section or call the company.

4  **Pay for your items.** Type in your order, address, and a credit card number or gift card number.

5  **Double-check your order** to make sure it's what you want. Then, **submit your order**.

6  **Print your order confirmation.**

Online Stores

Vocabulary

credit card	submit	web	confirmation	Help section
search engine	online	order	browse	online store

Conversation Questions

1. Why might it be easier for some people to shop online rather than go to a store?

   _____

2. Why would you need to use a search engine to help you find the store you are looking for?

   _____

3. What does it mean to "browse the web"?

   _____

4. Why should you double-check your order before submitting it?

   _____

5. Why do you use a credit or debit card to pay for items you buy online?

   _____

6. Why should you print an order confirmation for the items you purchased?

   _____

Extension Activities

1. Help students practice shopping online using actual websites. Have students practice checking out, but stop before they actually submit an order.

2. Ask students to search newspapers and flyers for store websites. Have students practice typing in the addresses and browsing through the products. Point out the Help section on each site.

3. Give students an item to search for using a search engine. When they find the item, have students print the page.

Transportation

Walk

Walking is the cheapest and healthiest form of transportation. Walking for just 30 minutes a day can make you healthier and improve your mood.

1  **Plan the route** you are going to walk.

2  **Tell someone when and where you are going** and when you will return from your walk.

3  **Dress appropriately** for your walk. Wear athletic shoes and clothes that are light reflective.

4  **Bring a bottle of water** in case you get thirsty.

5 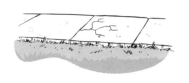 **Walk on the sidewalk.** If there is no sidewalk, walk along the side of the road facing traffic, so you can see oncoming cars.

6  **Return home** at the time you set.

#BK-376 Functional Sequencing • ©2010 Super Duper® Publications • www.superduperinc.com • 1-800-277-8737

Walk

Vocabulary

return	route	improve	thirsty	exercise
cheap	sidewalk	travel	healthy	mood

Conversation Questions

1. Why is it important to tell someone the route you will be walking and an approximate time you will return?

   _____

2. What makes walking a great way to travel short distances?

   _____

3. How do you think walking can improve your mood?

   _____

4. Why is it important to wear comfortable clothing and shoes on your walk?

   _____

5. How does walking make you healthier?

   _____

6. When might people choose not to walk to their destination?

   _____

Extension Activities

1. Take students on a walk around the school or on neighboring streets. Have them write down the things they see while on the walk.

2. Tie in the lesson for walking with the lesson for crossing the street (pages 78–79). Ask students to brainstorm their own sequence for safely crossing the street.

3. Ask students to research how walking is a great form of exercise and how it improves the body's health.

Bicycle

Bicycles have two wheels and move by pedaling. People ride bicycles for fun, health, and work. Bicycles are great because they are easy to park!

1  **Learn safety rules** for riding a bicycle as well as hand signals to tell people which way you will turn.

2  **Tell someone when and where you are going** and when you will return from your bicycle ride.

3  **Dress appropriately** for a bicycle ride. Wear athletic shoes and clothes that are light reflective.

4  **Put on a helmet and other safety equipment** you need.

5  **Bring a bottle of water** in case you get thirsty.

6  **Return home** at the time you set.

#BK-376 Functional Sequencing • ©2010 Super Duper® Publications • www.superduperinc.com • 1-800-277-8737

Bicycle

Vocabulary

bicycle	helmet	water bottle	hand signals	rules
route	appropriate	equipment	reflectors	park

Conversation Questions

1. Why should bicycle riders know hand signals for turning left or right and for slowing down?

   _____

2. Why should bicycle riders wear helmets?

   _____

3. How do reflectors and reflective clothing help keep a bicycle rider safe?

   _____

4. Why should you tell someone where you are going and the route you are taking to get there?

   _____

5. What should car drivers do when they get behind someone on a bicycle?

   _____

6. Why should you take a bottle of water with you on a bicycle ride?

   _____

Extension Activities

1. Find a copy of rules for bicycle safety and for bicycle riding on the street. Review rules with students. Assign students rules to draw (signaling a right turn, traffic laws, etc.). Post rules in the classroom.

2. Invite a local police officer/highway department worker to speak to the class on bicycle safety.

3. Bring in bicycle safety equipment. Have students practice putting on a helmet, knee pads, elbow pads, etc.

Car

Cars are a popular way to travel. Cars can seat two people or more! Remember to always wear your seat belt in the car.

1  **Open the car door.**

2  **Get in and have a seat.**

3  **Make sure your hands and feet are inside the car.**

4  **Shut the car door.**

5  **Buckle your seat belt.**

6  **Adjust the seat belt** so that it fits snuggly against your body.

#BK-376 Functional Sequencing • ©2010 Super Duper® Publications • www.superduperinc.com • 1-800-277-8737

Car

Vocabulary

seat belt	lock	buckle	comfortable	maintain
adjustments	trunk	gas	necessary	popular

Conversation Questions

1. Why do you think cars are the most popular form of transportation?

   _____

2. Why should the driver check the gas gauge before driving?

   _____

3. How do seat belts protect the driver and the passengers?

   _____

4. Why should the driver plan a route and the stops to make along the way?

   _____

5. Why should you lock the doors after getting into the car?

   _____

6. How are cars safer now than they used to be?

   _____

Extension Activities

1. Have students practice Steps 2–5 on page 110 in a mock car in the classroom.

2. Using copies of a road map, have students plot a route from your town to another town. Ask students to estimate how long it will take to drive, how much gas it will take, and star the places they would like to stop on the way.

3. Have students choose cars from ads in newspapers or magazines. Ask them to cut out the cars and glue them onto a poster board. Have students list the safety and environmental features of their cars.

School Bus

When riding the school bus, safety comes first. Always stay in your seat and keep your feet out of the aisle. Never put your head or hands out the bus windows. Listen to the bus driver at all times.

1  **Arrive at the bus stop** at least five minutes before the bus arrives.

2  **Wait quietly** for your bus to arrive.

3  If you have to cross the street to get on the bus, **look at the bus driver and wait for his or her signal**.

4  When the bus driver signals you, **look both ways and cross the street**.

5  **When the door opens, carefully get on the bus** one person at a time.

6  **Find a seat and sit quietly.**

#BK-376 Functional Sequencing • ©2010 Super Duper® Publications • www.superduperinc.com • 1-800-277-8737

School Bus

Vocabulary

bus stop	signal	school	rider	quiet
driver	students	arrive	wait	safety

Conversation Questions

1. Why do some students ride a bus to school?

_____

2. Why should you go to your bus stop a few minutes early?

_____

3. Why should students not play or horse around at a bus stop?

_____

4. Why should students talk very quietly while riding the bus?

_____

5. When can you get on the bus?

_____

6. Why should you keep your feet out of the aisle of the bus?

_____

Extension Activities

1. Arrange chairs like the inside of the school bus. One student pretends to be the driver while other students practice getting on the bus, talking quietly, listening to the bus driver's instructions, then exiting the bus safely.

2. Ask students to make a class list of rules for meeting, riding, and exiting the bus safely.

3. Ask a school bus driver to talk to students about bus safety. Let them board the bus and learn to exit the bus safely in case of an emergency. Students follow the bus driver's instructions.

City Bus

You will need to find information about the bus route, where the bus stops, and how much it costs to plan your ride.

City Bus Phone Number: _____

City Bus Website: _____

1  **Arrive at the bus stop** at least five minutes before the bus arrives.

2  **Check the sign on the bus.** Make sure it is going where you want to go.

3  **When the door opens, carefully get on the bus** one person at a time.

4  **Put your bus fare into the tin** at the front of the bus.

5  **Find a seat and sit quietly.**

6  **Keep an eye out for your stop.** You may need to push a button or pull a cord to let the bus driver know where you need to stop.

Transportation

#BK-376 Functional Sequencing • ©2010 Super Duper® Publications • www.superduperinc.com • 1-800-277-8737

City Bus

Vocabulary

schedule	driver	map	cord	similarity
difference	fare	pamphlet	button	depart

Conversation Questions

1. **What is a bus route?**

   _____

2. **Where do you go to meet the bus?**

   _____

3. **Why should you check the time that a bus arrives or departs before you go to the bus stop?**

   _____

4. **Why do you pay a fare to ride the city bus?**

   _____

5. **Why does the city provide maps and pamphlets of the different routes of city buses?**

   _____

6. **What should you do if you see a place where you need the bus driver to stop?**

   _____

Extension Activities

1. Discuss with students the environmental benefits of using mass transit.

2. Give each student a section of a city map and a map of the bus routes. Give students beginning and ending destinations and ask them to plan which bus(es) they will take and how much the fare will be. Another option is to do this activity as a class with large maps.

3. Research a bus company in your area. Look at the fares, times, and bus stops. Have students find the bus stop that is closest to their homes, schools, favorite restaurants, etc.

Taxi

You will need to find information about the taxi, how much it costs, and how many passengers can ride at one time.

Taxi Phone Number: _____

Taxi Website: _____

1	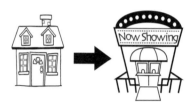	**Know the address** of where you are and where you want to go.
2		**Call the taxi company.** Tell them you need a taxi at the address where you are.
3		When the taxi arrives, **open the back door**.
4		**Get in and have a seat.**
5		**Tell the taxi driver where you want to go.**
6		When you arrive at your destination, **pay the amount on the meter and tip the taxi driver**.

#BK-376 Functional Sequencing • ©2010 Super Duper® Publications • www.superduperinc.com • 1-800-277-8737

Taxi

Vocabulary

taxi	destination	passenger	driver	meter
fare	luggage	address	tip	taxi company

Conversation Questions

1. Why do you need to tell the taxi company the address of where you are?

   _____

2. What should you tell the driver when you get into the taxi?

   _____

3. What should you do before you tell the driver where you want to go?

   _____

4. How can you find out about how much your fare will be before the taxi arrives?

   _____

5. Why should you make sure you have enough money for the ride?

   _____

6. Why should you tip the driver after paying the fare shown on the meter?

   _____

Extension Activities

1. Ask students to discuss reasons people may choose to call a taxi over driving or walking (weather, short distance, convenience, no parking).

2. Ask students to research taxi companies in the area. Look at the charges per mile and surcharge per passenger rates. Discuss the charges to ride in a taxi and why students should always know they have enough money for the ride before they go.

3. Ask students to discuss the differences between a taxi and a city bus. List reasons why you would choose one or the other.

Train

Bring reading materials or games to help pass the time on the train. Pay close attention to what the conductor tells you.

1  **Arrive at the train station** at least 45 minutes before the train departs.

2  **Bring your ticket or enough money to buy a ticket** when you arrive.

3  **Wait quietly and listen** for your train's number or name to be called.

4  **Follow the conductor's instructions** to get onto the train. The conductor will tell you where to put your luggage.

5  **Find your seat, sit quietly, and wait** for the conductor to take your ticket.

6  **Listen for the conductor to call out your stop.** Gather your things and wait for instructions from the conductor.

#BK-376 Functional Sequencing • ©2010 Super Duper® Publications • www.superduperinc.com • 1-800-277-8737

Train

Vocabulary

arrive	ticket	load	station	passenger
depart	procedure	conductor	instructions	train

Conversation Questions

1. Why is traveling by train sometimes better than taking a taxi or driving?

   _____

2. Why should you arrive at least 45 minutes before the train departs?

   _____

3. Where can you buy train tickets?

   _____

4. Why do you think there are certain procedures for passengers to load the train?

   _____

5. What should you do to help pass the time while riding the train?

   _____

6. Who will take your ticket on the train?

   _____

Extension Activities

1. Help students find access to train schedules online. Look at costs, destinations, and services offered to passengers. Have students choose destinations and try to determine how much money they will need to take their trips.

2. Research "sleeping cars." Have students discuss if they would spend the night on a train and what they think it would be like.

3. Ask students what the advantages may be going cross country on a train versus riding in a car or bus. List advantages/disadvantages, if there are any, on a class chart for all to see.

Airplane

Always bring a picture ID with you to the airport. You will need to show it several times before you board the plane. Make sure your name, address, and phone number are on all of your luggage. You will need a passport if you are flying out of the country

1  **Arrive at the airport** at least 90 minutes before the plane departs.

2  **Go to the ticket counter** of the airline you will be flying on.

3  **Show the attendant your ID** to check-in. The attendant will take all of your luggage except for carryons.

4  **Go through the security check.** You may have to take off your shoes and put everything from your pockets into a bin to be x-rayed.

5  As your personal items go through the x-ray machine, you will be required to **step through a metal detector**.

6  **Proceed to your gate and follow boarding procedures.**

#BK-376 Functional Sequencing • ©2010 Super Duper® Publications • www.superduperinc.com • 1-800-277-8737

Airplane

Vocabulary

airplane	gate	security	passport	connection
carryon	ID	board	luggage	metal detector

Conversation Questions

1. Why must you bring a picture ID with you to the ticket counter when you check-in?

   _____

2. Why should you arrive at the airport 90 minutes before your plane departs?

   _____

3. Why do passengers give their luggage to airline attendants during check-in?

   _____

4. Why must passengers go through a security check before proceeding to their gate?

   _____

5. What is a passport, and why must passengers have one to visit other countries?

   _____

6. Why do airlines limit what you can take on the plane and what you can keep at your seat?

   _____

Extension Activities

1. Help students understand why flying is expensive. Ask students to choose a faraway place they would like to go. Using a search engine, find an airline that flies to that place. Show students the cost, connections, and procedures for passengers listed on the website.

2. Research security procedures online for all major airlines. Discuss with students the reason for each procedure.

3. Ask students to compare the amount of time it would take to drive to a destination instead of flying.

Boat/Ferry

Ferries and boats carry groups of people and sometimes their cars across bodies of water. Some boats serve food and drinks. Passengers may stand or sit on the deck or stay inside.

Reference: http://www.ehow.com/how_2062461_travel-ferry-washington.html

1  **Arrive at the port** at least 20 minutes before the boat leaves.

2  **Bring your ticket or enough money to buy a ticket** when you arrive.

3  **Follow loading procedures** for boarding the boat or ferry.

4  **Find a seat and sit quietly.**

5  If you take a car on the boat, **remember to lock the doors** if you leave to go to one of the decks.

6  **Enjoy the ride!**

#BK-376 Functional Sequencing • ©2010 Super Duper® Publications • www.superduperinc.com • 1-800-277-8737

Boat/Ferry

Vocabulary

ferry	bridge	boarding	port	reading materials
deck	ride	procedures	boat	pass the time

Conversation Questions

1. Where do you go to get on a ferry or boat?

   _____

2. Why do you think there are procedures for loading passengers and cars onto a ferry?

   _____

3. Why do you think some ferries are free to ride and for others you need a ticket?

   _____

4. Why do some people choose to take a ferry if there is a bridge available to drive on?

   _____

5. Why must passengers follow rules while riding on a ferry or boat?

   _____

6. What is the difference between a ferry and a boat?

   _____

Extension Activities

1. Ask students to discuss why they think ferries are still in use (as opposed to building more bridges or taking other public transport).

2. Ask students to research different ferries still in operation throughout the U.S. Find lists of rules, procedures, schedules, and fares. Plot ferry findings on a map. Compare the ferry operations and their geographic locations.

3. Research the history of ferries and ferry ports. Explore why these ferries were such an advancement of transportation in the early settlements of the U.S.

Motorcycle

Motorcycles can be very dangerous. Always get your parents' permission before getting on a motorcycle. Make sure you know and trust the driver and that you wear protective gear.

1  **Dress appropriately** for a motorcycle ride. Wear long pants and long sleeves.

2  **Put on protective gear** including a leather jacket, sunglasses or goggles, and a helmet.

3  **Let the driver get on** the motorcycle first.

4  Once the driver is on, **swing your leg over the motorcycle and sit down**.

5  **Follow all of the driver's directions.**

6  **Hold on and be safe.**

#BK-376 Functional Sequencing • ©2010 Super Duper® Publications • www.superduperinc.com • 1-800-277-8737

Motorcycle

Vocabulary

protective	rules	permission	driver	directions
helmet	rider	goggles	gear	ride

Conversation Questions

1. Why must motorcycle drivers and riders wear protective gear?

   _____

2. What are some differences between a motorcycle and a car?

   _____

3. Why should motorcycle drivers and riders wear glasses or goggles?

   _____

4. What can happen if your feet get too close to the wheels of the motorcycle?

   _____

5. Why should the driver of the motorcycle get on before the rider?

   _____

6. What kind of road rules must motorcycle drivers follow?

   _____

Extension Activities

1. Ask students to discuss the dangers the drivers of motorcycles might encounter in comparison to drivers of trucks and cars.

2. Discuss unsafe driving conditions for a motorcycle and for a car.

3. Ask students to draw a picture of a motorcycle and the safety gear someone should wear while riding one.

Entertainment

Movie Theater

Look in the newspaper or online for movies that are playing near you and the showtimes. Arrive at least 10 minutes before showtime.

1  **Wait in line** to buy a ticket.

2  **Tell the cashier the movie and showtime you would like to buy a ticket for.**

3  **Pay the cashier** and take your change and your ticket.

4  **Give your ticket to the usher.**

5  **Follow the usher's directions** to the theater where your movie is playing.

6  **Find a seat and sit quietly.**

#BK-376 Functional Sequencing • ©2010 Super Duper® Publications • www.superduperinc.com • 1-800-277-8737

Movie Theater

Vocabulary

movie	online	newspaper	showtime	ticket
theater	seat	usher	previews	credits

Conversation Questions

1. Why should you arrive at least 10 minutes before a movie starts?

2. What should you tell the cashier when you are buying a ticket?

3. Why do you need to sit quietly during a movie?

4. What should you do if you have to go to the restroom during a movie?

5. Why do you need to look in the newspaper or online before going to a theater?

6. Who gives you directions as to which theater is showing your movie?

Extension Activities

1. Discuss with students why movies have ratings. Ask students to name movies and the ratings they have (G, PG, PG-13, R).

2. Theaters show previews before a movie starts. Ask students to list three reasons theaters show previews.

3. Lots of people work to make a movie. Ask students to name as many jobs as they can that need to be done to finish a movie. Compare students' list to the credits at the end of movies.

Zoo

The zoo can be a fun, but dangerous place. Remember, do not feed the animals or stick your hands or feet into the cages. Follow all rules while you are at the zoo!

1  **Wait in line** to buy a ticket.

2  **Tell the cashier you would like to buy a ticket.**

3  **Pay the cashier** and take your change and your ticket.

4  **Ask for a map of the zoo.**

5  **Give your ticket to the ticket collector.**

6  **Follow the signs or the map** to find the animals you want to see.

#BK-376 Functional Sequencing • ©2010 Super Duper® Publications • www.superduperinc.com • 1-800-277-8737

Zoo

Vocabulary

zoo	cage	animal	dangerous	food source
map	signs	rules	aquarium	habitat

Conversation Questions

1. Why might you need a map of the zoo?

   _____

2. Why shouldn't you feed the animals?

   _____

3. Why shouldn't you put your hands or feet into an animal's cage?

   _____

4. What kinds of animals are in the zoo?

   _____

5. What should you follow to get to a particular area of the zoo?

   _____

6. What is the difference between a zoo and a petting zoo?

   _____

Extension Activities

1. Animals at the zoo live in areas that resemble their native habitats. Ask students to draw different animal habitats at the zoo.

2. Some animals live in cages, some in aquariums, and some in fenced areas. Ask students to sort zoo animals into the different places they are kept.

3. Ask students to name their favorite zoo animals. Assist them in researching the animals. Search for native habitats, food sources, and other interesting information. Allow students to share and post the research they collect.

Swimming Pool

Remember to bring sunscreen, your bathing suit, a towel, and toys to the pool. Never swim alone. Never dive into shallow water. Do not swim in someone else's pool without their permission and supervision.

1  **Wait in line** for the pool attendant.

2  **Show the pool attendant your membership card.**

3  **Find a spot to put your things** while you are swimming.

4  **Make sure you know where the lifeguard is** before you get into the pool.

5  **Get into the pool. Don't splash others, and follow all pool rules.**

6  **When you get out, dry off** before leaving the pool area.

#BK-376 Functional Sequencing • ©2010 Super Duper® Publications • www.superduperinc.com • 1-800-277-8737

Swimming Pool

Vocabulary

hours	pool	membership	rules	lifeguard
splash	swim	attendant	sunscreen	bathing suit

Conversation Questions

1. What do you wear to go into the pool?

_____

2. Where does the lifeguard sit?

_____

3. Why is it important to always wear sunscreen?

_____

4. Why should you never swim alone?

_____

5. Why should you never dive into shallow water?

_____

6. What are some rules you should follow in the pool area?

_____

Extension Activities

1. Discuss with students what a lifeguard does. Ask students to draw a picture of a pool and where the lifeguard sits.

2. As a class, brainstorm and write on the board as many pool rules as possible.

3. Discuss with students the importance of wearing sunscreen and what can happen to skin over time when it's not protected.

Bowling Alley

Bowling is a fun activity and you can bowl whether it's sunny or rainy outside! The point of bowling is to roll a ball down a lane and knock over as many pins as you can. The more pins you knockdown, the higher your score!

1  **Wait in line for the clerk.**

2  **Tell the clerk your shoe size** so he or she can give you bowling shoes to wear. You must wear socks with bowling shoes.

3  **Go to the lane** the clerk assigns you.

4  **Pick a ball** from the turnstile or the shelf. Make sure it is not too heavy for you to lift.

5  **Bowl your ten frames.** The machine at your alley keeps the scores for you and the players on your team.

6  **Return your bowling shoes and pay the clerk** for the games you played.

Bowling Alley

Vocabulary

alley	weight	assign	appropriate	pins
frame	lane	turnstile	sportsmanship	clerk

Conversation Questions

1. What kind of weather can you bowl in? Why?

   _____

2. Where do you roll the bowling ball?

   _____

3. How many pins are standing at the end of the alley?

   _____

4. Why must you wear the bowling shoes the clerk gives you?

   _____

5. Why must you always wear socks with your bowling shoes?

   _____

6. What keeps everyone's scores during the bowling game?

   _____

Extension Activities

1. Set up a bowling alley in your classroom and let students play.

2. Discuss the importance of why bowling alleys provide shoes for bowling. Compare the differences in regular shoes versus bowling shoes. Discuss why players must wear socks and how shoes are sanitized.

3. Discuss sportsmanship with students. Ask students why it is important to be a good sport and have them role-play how they should be good sports in bowling.

Fishing Pond

Some people fish for food and others for sport. Depending on where you are, you can keep the fish you catch and eat them. Other places have contests to see who can catch the biggest fish and then release them back into the water.

1  **Find a pond or lake for fishing.** Make sure fishing is allowed and you have permission to fish there.

2  **Carefully bait your hook.** You can use worms, crickets, or lures that look like small fish.

3  **Cast your line into the water** and wait quietly and patiently.

4  **When you feel a hard tug, reel in your line.**

5  If you have a fish on your hook, **carefully remove the fish**.

6  **Put the fish back into the pond or lake** or into a cooler filled with water.

#BK-376 Functional Sequencing • ©2010 Super Duper® Publications • www.superduperinc.com • 1-800-277-8737

Fishing Pond

Vocabulary

catch	salt water	pole	hook	cast
lure	freshwater	reel	tug	bait

Conversation Questions

1. **Why do people fish?**

   _____

2. **What kind of bait can you use to catch fish?**

   _____

3. **Where do you put the bait?**

   _____

4. **How do you know when you have caught a fish?**

   _____

5. **What do you do after you catch a fish?**

   _____

6. **Where do you go fishing?**

   _____

Extension Activities

1. Look up varieties of fish online. Sort them into those that live in freshwater and salt water.

2. Discuss with students what "fishing for sport" means. Have them look up local fishing contests and the records for the fish caught.

3. Give students fishing magazines and ask them to cut out pictures of fish and different kinds of bait. Ask students to categorize the fish under the type of bait they like.

Beach

Many people visit the beach for vacation or just for a day of fun. Pack plenty of water, food, towels, and sunscreen. If you have a beach umbrella, bring it along for some shade.

1  **Dress appropriately for the beach.** Remember to bring towels for drying off and plenty of sunscreen.

2  **Pick a spot on the beach** to set up for the day. Lay out your towels and put up your umbrella if you brought one.

3  **Apply sunscreen to your face and body** before you play or swim.

4  **Tell someone where you are going** and what you are going to do. Do not go swimming without a partner.

5  **Be sure to drink plenty of water** and eat snacks throughout your time at the beach.

6  **Reapply sunscreen** after you go swimming each time.

#BK-376 Functional Sequencing • ©2010 Super Duper® Publications • www.superduperinc.com • 1-800-277-8737

Beach

Vocabulary

visit	swimming	sunscreen	towels	food
water	umbrella	bathing suit	partner	vacation

Conversation Questions

1. **Why do people go to the beach?**

   _____

2. **What kinds of things do people do at the beach?**

   _____

3. **Why should you apply sunscreen after swimming?**

   _____

4. **Why should you always have a swimming partner?**

   _____

5. **Why should you drink plenty of water at the beach?**

   _____

6. **What kinds of things should you take to the beach?**

   _____

Extension Activities

1. Some beaches have lifeguards, some don't. Discuss with students the similarities and differences in rules when there is and isn't a lifeguard at the beach.

2. Have students draw pictures of the beach and what they like to do there. Discuss the pictures with the class and then post them around the room.

3. Discuss with students the importance of wearing sunscreen and what happens later in life if you don't take care of your skin.

Sporting Event

Look in the newspaper or online for sports teams that are playing near you and the game times. Arrive at least 20 minutes before the event begins.

1  **Wait in line** to buy a ticket.

2  **Tell the cashier the section of seats you want a ticket for.**

3  **Pay the cashier** and take your change and your ticket.

4  **Give your ticket to the ticket collector.**

5  **Follow the usher's directions** to the section where your seat is.

6  **Find your seat and enjoy the sporting event!**

#BK-376 Functional Sequencing • ©2010 Super Duper® Publications • www.superduperinc.com • 1-800-277-8737

Sporting Event

Vocabulary

schedule	newspaper	team	online	prices
ticket	usher	seat	event	sell

Conversation Questions

1. How do you find out where sporting events are being held?

   _____

2. What are your favorite sports teams?

   _____

3. Why do sports teams sell tickets to the public?

   _____

4. Why should you arrive at least 20 minutes before an event begins?

   _____

5. How do you know where to find your seat?

   _____

6. What kinds of sports teams are in your area?

   _____

Extension Activities

1. Help students find schedules of sports teams in the area through a newspaper or online. Discuss the information provided like time, place, teams, etc.

2. Ask students to role-play buying a ticket and attending a sporting event. One student can be the attendee, another the cashier, etc.

3. Help students create t-shirts supporting their favorite sports team. Cut poster boards in the shape of t-shirts and have students decorate them for their favorite teams.

Concert

Musicians travel all over the world to perform concerts. Look in the newspaper or online for musicians that are playing near you. Look for the concert dates, times, and venues.

1  **Purchase your ticket ahead of time.** You can purchase online or by calling the venue where the concert will be held.

2  **Wait in line** at the box office to pick up your ticket.

3  **Tell the cashier your name** and he or she will give you your ticket.

4  **Give your ticket to the ticket collector.**

5  **Follow the usher's directions** to your seat.

6  **Find your seat and enjoy the concert!**

#BK-376 Functional Sequencing • ©2010 Super Duper® Publications • www.superduperinc.com • 1-800-277-8737

Entertainment

Concert

Vocabulary

concert	venue	usher	poster	perform
ticket	box office	musician	date	price

Conversation Questions

1. Where should you look to find concerts that are near you?

   _____

2. Where do musicians perform concerts?

   _____

3. Whom should you give your ticket to at the concert?

   _____

4. How do you know where your seat is?

   _____

5. How can you buy a ticket?

   _____

6. Which concerts would you like to go to?

   _____

Extension Activities

1. Have students create a poster announcing a concert date for a musician. Go over the important information to include. Display posters around the classroom.

2. Give students newspapers, or let them go online to search for concerts. Have them identify the important information about concerts like venues, ticket prices, dates, etc.

3. Collaborate with the music teacher and have your class help with the next school concert. Your students can create tickets, pass them out, be the ushers, make signs, etc.

Theater

Theaters are places where actors perform plays on a stage. Plays can be performed by professional actors or students. Be sure to reserve your ticket ahead of time and arrive at the theater at least 20 minutes before the performance begins.

1  **Reserve your ticket ahead of time.** You can reserve online or by calling the theater where the play will be held.

2  **Wait in line** at the box office to pick up your ticket.

3  **Tell the cashier your name** and he or she will give you your ticket.

4  **Pay the cashier** and take your change and your ticket.

5  **Give your ticket to the usher.**

6  **Follow the usher's directions** to your seat.

#BK-376 Functional Sequencing • ©2010 Super Duper® Publications • www.superduperinc.com • 1-800-277-8737

Theater

Vocabulary

play	perform	actor	audience	applaud
ticket	theater	reserve	directions	intermission

Conversation Questions

1. **What are plays?**

   _____

2. **Where are plays performed?**

   _____

3. **Where should you look to find plays near you?**

   _____

4. **How can you get a ticket to a play?**

   _____

5. **Why should you applaud when the play is over?**

   _____

6. **How should you behave while the play is performed?**

   _____

Extension Activities

1. Longer plays will have an intermission. Explain to your students what an intermission is and discuss what they should do during an intermission.

2. Use a book with short, simple plays for the students to act out in class. Assign students roles in the play. Other students can be the box office attendants, ushers, and audience members.

3. Discuss the rules for theater etiquette. Discuss clapping, talking, getting up from your seat, etc.

Miniature Golf

Miniature golf is a fun game! The goal is to use a golf club called a putter to hit a golf ball into the hole at the end of the green. Start at green #1 and take turns with other players all the way to the end of green #18.

1  **Pay the cashier** and take your change.

2  **Choose a putter and a golf ball.** Everyone playing should pick a different color golf ball.

3 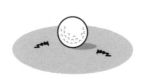 **Place the ball at the beginning of the green.**

4  **Swing your putter to hit the ball.** Hit the ball once, then give another player a turn.

5  **Continue to hit the ball until it goes into the hole** at the end of the green.

6 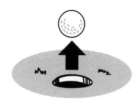 **Pick the ball out of the hole and continue to the next green.**

#BK-376 Functional Sequencing • ©2010 Super Duper® Publications • www.superduperinc.com • 1-800-277-8737

Miniature Golf

Vocabulary

golf	putter	green	golf ball	swing
hole	win	similarity	difference	club

Conversation Questions

1. How do you play miniature golf?

   _____

2. Why do you choose a ball that is a different color than everyone else's?

   _____

3. Where do you place the ball at the start of each hole?

   _____

4. What happens at the end of each hole?

   _____

5. How do you know who wins the game?

   _____

6. Whom should you ask for help, if you need any, on the miniature golf course?

   _____

Extension Activities

1. Ask students to research the history and rules of golf and miniature golf. Ask groups of students to put together lists of similarities and differences between the two games.

2. Have the class design their own nine-hole miniature golf course. Assign students to groups and each group designs their own hole. Students should decide which order the holes should go in. Display the course in its entirety around the classroom.

3. Have students practice playing miniature golf on a makeshift golf course on the playground.

School

Preparing for the Day

Listen to and follow the morning routine your teacher has for you. Most routines follow a pattern of unpacking your materials, waiting for instructions, and completing a morning activity before the bell rings.

1 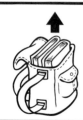 **Unpack your backpack.**

2  **Put items from your backpack where they belong.**

3  **Hang up your backpack and coat** where they belong.

4  **Sharpen your pencils** or take out your pens and prepare to work.

5  **Begin the morning activity** your teacher has prepared for you.

6 **Listen to the roll call.**

Preparing for the Day

Vocabulary

routine	pattern	sharpen	items	unpack
prepare	activity	prepare	roll call	backpack

Conversation Questions

1. Why do you think each teacher has a morning routine for his or her class?

   _____

2. What is good about having a morning routine at school?

   _____

3. What is the first thing you should do when you get to school?

   _____

4. Why should you sharpen your pencils before beginning your morning activity?

   _____

5. Why do you think teachers have students complete a morning activity before the bell rings?

   _____

6. Why is it good to prepare for the school day before it begins?

   _____

Extension Activities

1. Post the morning routine in the classroom. Have students follow the six steps in the "Preparing for the Day" activity on page 150 each morning.

2. Discuss other routines that may take place during the school day such as entering classrooms, walking in the hall, using the restroom, buying lunch, etc.

3. Discuss routines students may follow at home such as getting ready for school, setting the table, or doing laundry.

School

Roll Call

At the very beginning of the school day, the teacher may call out each name on the class roll to see if a student is present or absent. Roll call is the way the teacher keeps a record of how many days each student misses school.

1  **Sit quietly in your seat.**

2 **Listen to the teacher calling names** from the roll.

3  When the teacher calls your name **say, "Here" or "Present."**

4  **Continue to sit quietly** until the teacher finishes roll call.

5  **If you were absent the day before, give the teacher your excuse** after he or she finishes roll call.

6  Once you give the teacher your note, **return to your seat**.

#BK-376 Functional Sequencing • ©2010 Super Duper® Publications • www.superduperinc.com • 1-800-277-8737

Roll Call

School

Vocabulary

beginning	continue	roll	excuse	names
present	here	absent	note	record

Conversation Questions

1. What does the teacher do at the very beginning of the school day?

2. What is a class roll?

3. Why does the teacher need to know who is present or absent from school?

4. What should you say when the teacher calls your name?

5. What should you do after the teacher calls your name?

6. Why do you bring a note to the teacher if you were absent the day before?

Extension Activities

1. Discuss why teachers keep a log of when students are absent. Discuss the number of times students can miss school.

2. Discuss the dangers of teachers not calling roll especially if a student is absent. Most schools call a student's home when he/she is absent to make sure the absence is valid and the student is not skipping school.

3. Discuss why students must bring a note or "excuse" for their absence from a doctor or a parent.

Getting in Line

When an entire class must move from one place to another, students get into a line. A line helps keep students in an orderly group that the teacher can easily monitor.

1  When the teacher asks students to line up, **find a place in line**.

2  **Keep your hands to yourself.**

3  **Stand quietly** and wait for the teacher's instructions.

4  **Don't stand too close to the person in front of you.**

5  When the line begins moving, **follow the leader**.

6  **Walk quietly in line.**

#BK-376 Functional Sequencing • ©2010 Super Duper® Publications • www.superduperinc.com • 1-800-277-8737

Getting in Line

Vocabulary

entire	line up	monitor	yourself	line
orderly	leader	hands	listen	follow

Conversation Questions

1. What does the teacher mean when he or she asks students to line up?

   _____

2. Why should you stand quietly while waiting in line?

   _____

3. Why should you not stand too close to the person in front of you?

   _____

4. What should you do when the line begins moving?

   _____

5. What would the line be like if people stood too close to each other and were talking?

   _____

6. What happens if you do not follow the leader when the line is moving?

   _____

Extension Activities

1. Ask students to practice getting in line. Ask one student to not follow the rules while in line. Discuss with students the impact this person had on the rest of the line. Discuss how disorderly moving students would be if there were no lines. Discuss other hallway rules.

2. Ask students to list all of the places in school they get in line to go to.

3. Discuss ways the teacher could ask students to line up by (birthday month, alphabetical order, eye color).

Answering Questions

Being able to answer questions at school lets you and the teacher know if you understand what you are learning. You must pay close attention to the lessons, do your work, and ask the teacher to explain what you may not understand.

School

1 **Listen closely** to the teacher's lesson.

2  When the teacher asks a question, **think about the answer**.

3  **Raise your hand when you know the answer** to the question. Do not shout out your answer.

4  **Wait quietly** until the teacher calls your name.

5  **Tell the class your answer.**

6 **Continue listening** to the teacher's lesson.

#BK-376 Functional Sequencing • ©2010 Super Duper® Publications • www.superduperinc.com • 1-800-277-8737

Answering Questions

Vocabulary

understand	answer	think	raise	explain
question	closely	shout	attention	lesson

Conversation Questions

1. Why does the teacher ask questions during a lesson?

   _____

2. Why should you pay close attention to each lesson?

   _____

3. Why should you think about the teacher's question before you answer it?

   _____

4. How do you let the teacher know you want to answer a question?

   _____

5. Why should you not shout out your answer?

   _____

6. What should you do if you don't understand something in the lesson?

   _____

Extension Activities

1. Make a list of questions that students should know the answers to. Have students practice raising their hands and waiting for the teacher to call on them. If a student shouts an answer, he/she loses the opportunity to play.

2. Play a question game. Teacher writes an item on a note card. Students must ask the teacher questions (by raising hands and taking turns) to determine what the item is.

3. Discuss with student why they should think about a question before trying to answer it. What happens when you blurt out an answer before thinking about the question?

Doing Homework

Homework reinforces what you learn in school. Make sure you complete your homework every night.

1 **Listen to the teacher** when he or she gives you a homework assignment.

2  **Write down the homework assignment** in your notebook or student planner.

3  **Work on your homework when you have free time** at school or at home.

4  **Ask an adult questions if you need help** with your homework.

5  **When you finish your homework, put it into your backpack.**

6  **Give your homework to your teacher** the next school day.

#BK-376 Functional Sequencing • ©2010 Super Duper® Publications • www.superduperinc.com • 1-800-277-8737

Doing Homework

Vocabulary

assignment	notebook	reinforce	teacher	homework
work	before	free time	planner	listen

Conversation Questions

1. **Why do students have to do homework?**

   _____

2. **Why should you write down your homework assignments?**

   _____

3. **Where should you write down your homework assignments?**

   _____

4. **When should you do your homework?**

   _____

5. **What should you do with your homework when you finish it?**

   _____

6. **Whom do you give your homework to on the next school day?**

   _____

Extension Activities

1. Determine one place in the classroom where the teacher will always post homework assignments. Have students designate a notebook or planner for writing down assignments.

2. Discuss with students the benefits of doing homework. Ask what makes good homework assignments; what makes homework assignments difficult; too long, too hard, too boring, etc.

3. Set aside a few minutes each day for students to write down homework assignments. Assign partners to check that the homework assignment is written down correctly and that the bookbag has all of the necessary materials.

Packing Your Backpack

Being ready for school means having everything you need. Check your list twice before you leave home.

1  **Unzip your backpack.**

2  **Put homework, notebooks, books, and pencils into your backpack.**

3  If you have gym class, **put gym clothes into your backpack**.

4  **Put your lunch bag on top of your books.**

5  **Pack your student ID.**

6  **Zip your backpack.**

#BK-376 Functional Sequencing • ©2010 Super Duper® Publications • www.superduperinc.com • 1-800-277-8737

Packing Your Backpack

Vocabulary

backpack	homework	gym	student ID	clothes
books	zip	unzip	list	pencils

Conversation Questions

1. Where should you put your pencils, books, and homework to go to school?

   _____

2. Why should you put your lunch on top of everything in your backpack?

   _____

3. When should you pack your backpack?

   _____

4. What else might you put into your backpack?

   _____

5. What should you do if you can't fit everything into your backpack?

   _____

6. What should you do if your backpack is too heavy to carry?

   _____

Extension Activities

1. If students do have gym class, ask them to list all of the items included with *Step 3: Packing Gym Clothes*.

2. Ask students to practice packing a backpack. Provide them with a backpack and supplies or allow them to use their own.

3. Give students store ads to browse and ask them to pick out different kinds of backpacks and make a list of the pros and cons of each.

Packing Your Lunch

Eating healthy is very important. Take good food with you to school. You will be more alert and learning will be easier when you eat right and stay healthy. Avoid packing sugary foods and snacks.

1  **Make a sandwich.**

2  **Put the sandwich into a plastic bag or container.**

3  **Choose a vegetable or fruit and a small snack.**

4  **Use a thermos for your beverage.** It will keep your drink cold.

5  **Put the food and thermos into your lunch bag.**

6  **Close the bag tightly.**

#BK-376 Functional Sequencing • ©2010 Super Duper® Publications • www.superduperinc.com • 1-800-277-8737

Packing Your Lunch

Vocabulary

lunch	sandwich	plastic bag	container	USDA
beverage	thermos	healthy	vegetables	fruit

Conversation Questions

1. What time do you eat lunch?

   _____

2. What should you put your sandwich in?

   _____

3. Why would you use a thermos?

   _____

4. What should you do if you have something hot to pack?

   _____

5. Where should you put your lunch after you pack it?

   _____

6. Why should you pack fruits and vegetables?

   _____

Extension Activities

1. Ask students to draw a healthy lunch. Have students share their pictures with the class and tell why they chose each item.

2. Have a lunchroom manager speak to the class about how lunch menus are created. Ask the manager to tell how each lunch menu must offer foods from each food group.

3. Discuss the USDA's (United States Department of Agriculture) current dietary guidelines. Have students list foods they eat and where they are in the guidelines. Discuss serving size and what is "too much."

Restroom Breaks

Try to take restroom breaks between classes, at recess, or at lunchtime; but don't be embarrassed to ask the teacher to be excused. The teacher understands that you may need to go at times other than a scheduled break.

School *(vertical side label)*

1 **Raise your hand.**

2  When the teacher calls on you **ask, "May I please use the restroom?"**

3  SCHOOL HALL PASS — When the teacher gives you permission, **take the hall pass**.

4  **Walk quietly to the restroom.** Don't run.

5  When you finish using the restroom, **walk quietly back to class**.

6  Enter the classroom quietly, return the hall pass, and **go back to your seat**.

#BK-376 Functional Sequencing • ©2010 Super Duper® Publications • www.superduperinc.com • 1-800-277-8737

Restroom Breaks

Vocabulary

restroom	raise	quietly	seat	wash
permission	classroom	enter	hall pass	dry

Conversation Questions

1. When should you use the restroom?

   _____

2. How do you let the teacher know you need his or her attention?

   _____

3. What should you ask the teacher when you need to use the restroom?

   _____

4. Why do students use a hall pass?

   _____

5. Why should you walk quietly to the restroom and not run?

   _____

6. Why should you enter the classroom quietly when you return from the restroom?

   _____

Extension Activities

1. Review scheduled restroom break times so students will make a habit of going to the restroom at these times. Encourage students to take advantage of the scheduled break and try to use the restroom even if it doesn't "feel like" they need to go.

2. Review restroom etiquette: flushing, washing hands, drying hands, etc. Talk about the health issues created by not washing hands.

3. Ask students to practice raising their hands, asking permission to use the restroom, taking the hall pass, and exiting the classroom quietly.

Field Trips

Field trips are planned activities that take place away from school. You may go to a park, zoo, or museum. These activities and trips may highlight information that you are learning in school.

School

1  Ask your parent or guardian to **fill out the permission slip** and sign it.

2  **Return the permission slip** to your teacher.

3  **Remember to bring money or a bagged lunch** the day of the field trip.

4 **Be kind to others and always listen to your teachers** when on a field trip.

5  **Stay close to your group**— never wander away on your own.

6  **Have fun!**

#BK-376 Functional Sequencing • ©2010 Super Duper® Publications • www.superduperinc.com • 1-800-277-8737

Field Trips

Vocabulary

field trip	parent	permission slip	group	museum
activity	guardian	wander	close	plan

Conversation Questions

1. What are field trips?

   _____

2. Why might your class take a field trip?

   _____

3. Where are some places students go on field trips?

   _____

4. Why do you need a parent's or guardian's permission to go on a field trip?

   _____

5. Why should you listen closely to your teachers on the field trip?

   _____

6. Why should you stay close to your group and not wander away on your own?

   _____

Extension Activities

1. Ask students to make a list of places they could visit that would reinforce what they are learning in school: animals-zoo, art-museum, reading-library, recycling-landfill.

2. Talk about the importance of parental/guardian permission when planning to go on a field trip. Discuss the permission slip and why it asks for certain information.

3. Plan a pretend field trip with your students. Go through the planning process with students, including arranging the trip transportation, permission slips, lunch, fees, appropriate clothing, etc.